Cambridge Elements ≡

Elements in the Philosophy of Religion
edited by
Yujin Nagasawa
University of Birmingham

GOD AND HUMAN FREEDOM

Leigh Vicens
Augustana University, South Dakota
Simon Kittle
University of Innsbruck

CAMBRIDGE
UNIVERSITY PRESS

CAMBRIDGE
UNIVERSITY PRESS

University Printing House, Cambridge CB2 8BS, United Kingdom

One Liberty Plaza, 20th Floor, New York, NY 10006, USA

477 Williamstown Road, Port Melbourne, VIC 3207, Australia

314–321, 3rd Floor, Plot 3, Splendor Forum, Jasola District Centre, New Delhi – 110025, India

79 Anson Road, #06–04/06, Singapore 079906

Cambridge University Press is part of the University of Cambridge.

It furthers the University's mission by disseminating knowledge in the pursuit of education, learning, and research at the highest international levels of excellence.

www.cambridge.org
Information on this title: www.cambridge.org/9781108457545
DOI: 10.1017/9781108558396

First published 2019

A catalogue record for this publication is available from the British Library.

ISBN 978-1-108-45754-5 Paperback
ISSN 2399-5165 (online)
ISSN 2515-9763 (print)

God and Human Freedom

Elements in the Philosophy of Religion

DOI: 10.1017/9781108558396
First published online: July 2019

Leigh Vicens
Augustana University, South Dakota
Simon Kittle
University of Innsbruck
Author for correspondence: Leigh Vicens, leigh.vicens@augie.edu

Abstract: This Element considers the relationship between the traditional view of God as all-powerful, all-knowing and wholly good on the one hand, and the idea of human free will on the other. It focuses on the potential threats to human free will arising from two divine attributes: God's exhaustive foreknowledge and God's providential control of creation.

Keywords: free will, God, divine foreknowledge, divine providence, the problem of evil

ISBNs: 9781108457545 (PB), 9781108558396 (OC)
ISSNs: 2399-5165 (online), 2515-9763 (print)

Contents

Introduction

Philosophical theorising about God often begins with the idea, made famous by Anselm, that God is the greatest possible being. On such a view, God must have all the 'great-making' properties, or perfections. Some of the properties often thought to be great-making include *omnipotence* (being all-powerful), *omniscience* (being all-knowing), *omnibenevolence* (being wholly good) and perfect freedom. This philosophical approach to God is known as *perfect being theology* and the present work is situated in that tradition. There are different ways of working this project out, but for the most part, the finer details do not concern us. That's because in what follows we are concerned, not with the internal coherence of the divine attributes, but with whether certain aspects of God's being and activity are compatible with human free will.

In contemporary philosophy free will is often defined as *the control required to be morally responsible*. Here 'control' is to be understood as *control over our decisions, actions and (some of) their consequences*. This definition is functionalist inasmuch as it identifies free will by the role it plays. Throughout this Element we combine this definition of free will with the substantive idea that free will consists in having a choice about something. One reason for starting with this substantive notion of free will is that it is intuitive: all of us, through making choices, direct our lives to some degree or other. From choosing what to have for breakfast to which hobby to take up – or from whom to vote for to which friendships to invest in – having choices about these things is prized, even when some such choices are tough to make.

Indeed, even when our freedom *of action* is curtailed – when, for example, we are forced to do or to undergo something we might not want to – freedom *of choice* often remains; when it does, such freedom can alter, and bestow value on, our experiences. Henri Nouwen captures this nicely in a book of spiritual reflections:

> Joy is what makes life worth living, but for many joy seems hard to find . . . [Yet] strange as it may sound, *we can choose* joy. Two people can be part of the same event, but one . . . may choose to trust that what happened, painful as it may be, holds a promise. The other may choose despair and be destroyed by it. What makes us human is precisely this freedom of choice. (1996: 37, emphasis added)

Moreover, making choices is often valued, not just because of the control over our lives it gives us, but also because in making choices we both *reveal something about* and *help to form* our identity as persons. As Dumbledore once explained to Harry Potter, "It is our choices, Harry, that show what we truly are, far more than our abilities" (Rowling 2015: 352).

Gary Watson goes so far as to say that a human "who never engaged in such activity [i.e. deciding] would be an agent only in a truncated sense" (2004b: 126). Watson's point here is that there is a significant form of human agency which depends on being able to make reasoned choices. Moreover, this form of agency plays a central role in our conception of ourselves. Tillmann Vierkant, Julian Kiverstein and Andy Clark note the practical importance of choice when they write that the idea that humans can make autonomous decisions is "absolutely central to many of our social institutions, from criminal responsibility to the markets, from democracies to marriage" (2013: 1).

Another reason for starting with this substantive, choice-based understanding of free will is that the most venerable theological puzzles concerning God and free will only arise – or at least, arise in their most difficult forms – given this understanding of free will. Thus, if the existence and nature of God can be shown to be compatible with *this* conception of free will, it is a safe bet that whatever the precise nature of free will turns out to be, it will be compatible with the existence and nature of God.

Free will, or freedom – in this work we use the terms interchangeably – is a significant topic in many areas of philosophy of religion and theology. Freedom is relevant to the doctrine of God first and foremost because it is usually seen as one of the great-making properties that God must possess. How we understand God's own freedom affects how we understand His activity in the world, and so informs statements of the doctrine of creation. The topic of God's freedom also impacts theological anthropology, especially in the Judeo-Christian tradition, according to which human beings are said to be made in the image of God. For many theorists, a key part of this idea is that humans were given some measure of free will because God Himself is free. Free will is also a central topic of concern in the Christian doctrine of salvation. That's because, according to the dominant view within the Western Church, humankind was subject to the Fall, an event through which evil entered human life, God's creation became disordered, and human beings became unable to restore themselves to their original state. On this view God must intervene to save humans and salvation is therefore seen as a free gift from God – an act of His free will. At the same time, however, Christian theology usually teaches that humans are responsible for their state of brokenness. These two facts combine to generate the problem of grace and free will. The Eastern tradition within Christianity does not have quite the same doctrine of the Fall, and so doesn't generate the same tension between grace and free will, but nevertheless has an important place for human freedom in its theology.[1]

---

[1] Most of those whose work we discuss write from within the Christian tradition, and some of their positions – such as those related to the issues of sin, grace and salvation – arise out of a commitment to Christian orthodoxy. This commitment is most evident in Section 2, since

This Element focuses on two topics regarding which human freedom has significant relevance for the theistic worldview. The first is the problem of divine foreknowledge. In brief the problem is as follows: if God knows in advance how we will make each choice we face in our lives, and God cannot be wrong (so that what He knows must come to pass), how can our choices be free? This problem, which has been debated for millennia, is fascinating in part because it touches upon many philosophically difficult topics: causation, time, the future, truth and knowledge – in addition, of course, to God and freedom. For this reason the problem still garners much attention today among both theist and atheist philosophers. This is the topic of Section 1.

In Section 2 we consider the relationship between divine providence and human freedom. We understand *divine providence* to be God's acting to realise His ends. We construe this broadly so as to include, to use traditional theological language, God's *preserving* in being everything He creates, His *concurrence* with created causes, His *general provision* for what He creates and His *special* or *particular actions* within history. Sometimes the former two concepts are treated as part of the doctrine of creation, and the latter two are grouped together as God's *governance* of creation. For convenience, we treat them all as aspects of divine providence. The worry that arises in connection with free will here is that if God has complete control over all He has created – if God is sovereign over absolutely everything that comes to pass (as would seem fitting) – then there appears to be little room for any human *agency* at all, let alone human *freedom*. The challenge, as many theist thinkers see it, is to work out a doctrine of providence which takes seriously human freedom (to secure human responsibility) while also doing justice to God's sovereignty and control over His creation.

1 Divine Foreknowledge and Human Freedom

1.1 The Problem of Divine Foreknowledge and Human Freedom

The problem of divine foreknowledge and human freedom can be stated informally as follows. God is omniscient, and so knows everything there is to know, including facts about the future. God is also infallible, and so cannot be mistaken in what He knows. This means that God has always known how everyone will decide and act at any future time. But if God has always known just how each person will decide in the future, then those future decisions appear to be necessary or fixed in some way. And if those decisions are necessary or

---

many of those writing on divine providence seek to do justice to various biblical texts and confessional creeds which speak to God's control over human affairs.

fixed, then they are not free, because someone makes a free decision only if she is able to decide otherwise.

This venerable philosophical problem has been discussed in the Western tradition for thousands of years and has generated a vast literature. Part of the reason for that, of course, is that it concerns a central aspect of the doctrine of God and is of interest to every generation of theists. But the philosophical puzzle is also intriguing, and attracts the attention of many non-theists, because it touches upon so many other topics of philosophy: truth, the future, time and temporal ontology, modality and, of course, free will.

The argument outlined in the first paragraph of this section is, at its core, an argument which aims to show that exhaustive divine foreknowledge and human free will are incompatible. We understand *the problem of divine foreknowledge and human free will* to be the problem of either (a) saying where the reasoning of that argument goes wrong, or (b) justifying the rejection of divine foreknowledge or human freedom. We call those who pursue the first strategy *foreknowledge compatibilists*: they think there is a flaw in the argument and that divine foreknowledge and human freedom are compatible.[2] Those who pursue the second strategy are *foreknowledge incompatibilists*: they defend the validity of the reasoning in the argument and so must reject either divine foreknowledge or free will.

Before formally stating the argument that is discussed in what follows, we lay out the argument's assumptions. The argument assumes that God exists and is essentially eternal, essentially omniscient and infallible. There are two ways of understanding God's eternality. The first is that God is temporal and exists at all times. The second is that God is atemporal in the sense that He is 'outside' of time and doesn't have any temporal properties. Sometimes writers reserve the term 'everlasting' to refer to the first notion and reserve the term 'eternal' to refer to the second. However, given that both 'everlasting' and 'eternal' are widely found in English translations of the Bible, we prefer to avoid associating these terms with technical concepts and instead simply to be explicit about the concepts in play. The argument presented in what follows assumes that God is eternal in the first sense: God is temporal and exists at all times. As we see in Section 1.2.5, one prominent way of resisting the argument is by rejecting this assumption.

---

[2] In the foreknowledge literature this position is often called *theological compatibilism*. However, the label 'theological compatibilism' is also used to describe the view that God's determining activity is compatible with human freedom. Since we discuss that position at length in the next section, we use the term 'foreknowledge compatibilism' for the compatibilist view discussed in this section.

Omniscience is the property of knowing the truth value of all propositions. Essential omniscience is the property of necessarily knowing the truth value of all propositions. Infallibility is the property of being unable to make any mistakes in one's beliefs (Zagzebski 1996: 4–5). Infallibility is not entailed by omniscience (because an omniscient being might be capable of losing its omniscience), but it is entailed by essential omniscience.

The argument assumes that future contingent propositions can be true prior to the times they are about. Future contingent propositions are propositions about contingent future states of affairs. For example, the propositions *that you will decide to have cereal for breakfast on January 1, 2042*, and *that the Green Party will win a UK general election in 2027* are, at the time of writing (2018), future contingents. The future contingent propositions relevant to the argument are, of course, those which involve future human decisions.

Finally, the argument appeals to the intuitive idea that certain facts about the past are, to use Nelson Pike's words, "fully accomplished" and "over and done with" (1970: 59). These are what we might intuitively think of as 'genuine' facts about the past. In the literature on foreknowledge and free will they are called *hard facts* about the past. All other facts are called *soft facts*. The following facts are – relative to our time of writing in 2018 – paradigm cases of hard facts:

> Paradigm hard facts relative to 2018
> Martin Luther posted his ninety-five theses to the door of the castle church of Wittenberg in 1517.
> Goran Ivanišević won Wimbledon in 2001.

It is very intuitive that hard facts such as these are now *fixed* in an important sense: no one has (now) the power to prevent these facts from being true; no one has (now) any choice about these matters. It is simply *too late* to do anything about them. Soft facts, by contrast, are not, relative to a given time, "over and done with", which is to say they are not, relative to that time, "temporally intrinsic" facts but are in part about other future times – they are "temporally relational" facts (see Todd 2013). As such, soft facts are not necessarily fixed in the sense given earlier. Suppose, for example, that it is now (in 2018, as we are writing this Element) true that you will choose to have cereal for breakfast on January 1, 2042. The fact that you will choose to have cereal for breakfast on January 1, 2042, is a soft fact because it is not (at the time of writing) over and done with. Moreover, this seems to be just the kind of thing that you do have control over: it's not too late for you to prevent your cereal eating. Not all soft facts which appear to be entirely (or mostly) about the future are like this, however. For example, the fact that the sun will rise on January 1, 2042, is a soft fact which does not appear to be under anyone's control. So, some soft facts are fixed too. Then again, some facts about the past – or at least, partially about the past – seem to be soft facts which are not fixed. Thus, while *Goran Ivanišević's winning of Wimbledon in 2001* is a hard fact, relative to our time of writing, the fact – and let us suppose it is a fact – that *Goran Ivanišević's 2001 Wimbledon win is the only winning of the men's Wimbledon title by a Croatian in the twenty-first century* is, relative to the time of writing, a soft fact. The latter fact is in part about each Wimbledon championship that is to be played in the twenty-first century and no doubt many (present and future) Croatian tennis players hope they have the power to prevent its truth. Some soft facts which are in part about the past do appear to be beyond anyone's control, however; for example, the fact – assuming it is a fact – that Sally had breakfast yesterday, exactly two days before a meteor impact on Pluto, is a soft fact that appears to be beyond anyone's control. The distinction between hard and soft facts is discussed further in Section 1.2.3 which considers a response to the argument – Ockhamism – based on this distinction. Section 1.2.4 considers a response to the argument which challenges the idea that hard facts about the past are fixed.

When some proposition p is true, and some person S is unable at t to act so as to make it false, we say that *S has no choice about* the truth of proposition p. We use what has come to be a fairly standard abbreviation for this idea, namely, '$N^S_t(p)$'. Thus,

$$N^S_t(p)$$

is short for

p and S has, at and after t, no choice about the fact that p.

To illustrate with a concrete example,

$$N^{David}_{2019}(\text{Goran Ivanišević won Wimbledon in 2001})$$

is short for

Goran Ivanišević won Wimbledon in 2001 and David has, in and after 2019, no choice about the fact that Goran Ivanišević won Wimbledon in 2001.

That's quite a mouthful, hence the 'N' abbreviation.

With that background in place we can now present the argument for the conclusion that divine foreknowledge and human freedom are incompatible. We use Pike's example of Jones's lawn mowing as our ordinary action, although we cast it in terms of Jones's *decision* to mow her lawn, rather than the mowing itself. Suppose, then, that it is true that at Saturday lunchtime (t3) Jones will decide to mow her lawn. Time t1 is some time before t2, which is itself a time before t3. The argument for the incompatibility of foreknowledge and free will runs as follows:[3]

(1) God believed at time t1 that Jones would decide at t3 to mow her lawn.

(2) N^{Jones}_{t2}(God believed at t1 that Jones would decide at t3 to mow her lawn).

(3) If $N^S_t(p)$ and $N^S_t(p$ entails $q)$, then $N^S_t(q)$.

(4) N^{Jones}_{t2}(God believed at t1 that Jones would decide at t3 to mow her lawn entails that Jones will decide at t3 to mow her lawn).

(5) N^{Jones}_{t2}(Jones will decide at t3 to mow her lawn).

(6) If N^{Jones}_{t2}(Jones will decide at t3 to mow her lawn), then Jones cannot decide to refrain from mowing her lawn.

(7) If Jones cannot decide to refrain from mowing her lawn, she does not at t3 decide to mow her lawn freely.

(8) Therefore, Jones does not at t3 decide to mow her lawn freely.

Clearly, there is nothing special about Jones deciding to mow her lawn, so the argument will generalise to all human decisions and actions. If sound, the argument establishes that divine foreknowledge of human decisions is incompatible with human freedom, a thesis we call *foreknowledge incompatibilism*. The version of the argument presented earlier yields a fatalistic conclusion. That is, it assumes that God is indeed omniscient and concludes – by establishing that foreknowledge and free will are incompatible – that free will does not exist. Few of those who defend the incompatibility of foreknowledge and free will, however, accept the fatalistic conclusion. Typically, they treat premise (1) as an assumption for an indirect proof and continue as follows:

(9) But, Jones will decide at t3 to mow her lawn freely.

(10) Therefore, (contrary to (1)), God did not believe at t1 that Jones would decide at t3 to mow her lawn.

In contrast, *foreknowledge compatibilists* hold that divine foreknowledge and free will are compatible and so are committed to (1) and must therefore reject one or more of the argument's other assumptions, premises or inferences. All the responses considered in what follows are compatibilist except for the open theist response discussed in Section 1.2.6.

---

[3] This argument is closely modelled on John Martin Fischer's (1989: 6) modal version of the argument.

1.2 Responses to the Argument

1.2.1 Alternative Views of Free Will

The argument for foreknowledge incompatibilism given earlier assumes that free will consists in having a choice about something. When an agent faces a *choice* or *decision* (we use the terms interchangeably), she has at least two options from among which she can select. Choice therefore entails the existence of what the contemporary literature calls *alternative possibilities*: possible alternative unfoldings of the world. (The existence of alternative possibilities does not entail choice, however, because there might be unfoldings of the world over which the agent herself has no control.) On this account of free will an agent, P, who faces a decision between A and B will decide freely only if (i) P is able to decide to A, and (ii) P is able to decide to B (where deciding to B might simply be deciding to refrain from A-ing).

This argument makes explicit use of this intuitive notion of free will in premise 7:

(7) If Jones cannot decide to refrain from mowing her lawn, she does not at t3 decide to mow her lawn freely.

As such, one way of dispatching the argument quickly and effectively is to reject this view of free will. The most straightforward way of doing so is to say that the kind of control required for moral responsibility – this, recall, is the functional definition of 'free will' given in the introduction – does not involve choice. There are many such accounts of free will. Take, for example, Thomas Hobbes's account. On his view an action is a behavioural event that is caused by a desire. And the agent herself is free in the execution of some action if there are no impediments to action that are extrinsic to the agent (Hobbes, Bramhall & Chappell 1999: 38). Having a choice about what one's desires are, or which way to realise one's desires, is simply not needed. Hobbes's view does not fare well once it is accepted that a person may be subject to internal factors that she does not endorse but that determine or even merely influence what she does; and since Freud, it has been widely accepted that a person may have desires of which she is completely unaware and may not want to have.

Contemporary non-choice-based accounts of free will tend, therefore, to be more sophisticated. One example is Harry Frankfurt's idea that freedom involves the alignment of a person's 'second-order' desires with her 'first-order' desires. First-order desires are desires for food, shelter etc. Second-order desires are desires about one's first-order desires. For example, to want to smoke is a first-order desire; to want to not want to smoke – i.e. to want to be free from any desire to smoke – is a second-order desire. The point is that you might want to smoke while also wanting to not have that desire to smoke. Frankfurt's (1971) suggestion was that a person is free when a first-order desire which she wants to have – i.e. for which she has a second-order desire – causes her to act.

On non-choice-based views of free will such as Hobbes's and Frankfurt's, free will is straightforwardly compatible with God's foreknowledge. While such accounts solve the problem of foreknowledge, we say very little about them here, for two reasons. First, we remain unconvinced that any non-choice-based account of free will captures the notion of control relevant to free will. As we've already noted, choice has immediate and obvious moral significance; it is implicated in all or almost all areas of human social life and practice. And it seems to us that the degree to which non-choice-based accounts of free will appear plausible is the degree to which they smuggle back in the notion of choice. To give just one example, critics of Frankfurt's early hierarchical account pointed out that there doesn't seem to be anything special about second-order desires which makes them authoritative for the agent. Why think that an agent's will – the first-order desire which moves her to act – is free if she has a second-order desire for that first-order desire? After all, just as an agent might have first-order desires she would rather not have, so an agent might have second-order desires she would rather not have. This is a question of *identification*: which desires are truly the agent's own? (See Stump (1996) for further discussion.) In a later paper responding to this question, Frankfurt suggested that a desire might become authoritative for a person when the person *makes a decision* to identify with that desire: "Through his action in deciding, he is responsible for the fact that the desire has become his own in a way in which it was not unequivocally his own before" (1988: 170). This might well solve the problem, but if so, it is only because the key notion of *decision* or *choice* has been reintroduced.

The second reason for not treating non-choice-based accounts in any depth is that, even if someone presented a non-choice-based account of free will that sufficed for moral responsibility, we would still care to some degree about the freedom to do otherwise. That's because, as already stated, in our ordinary deliberation and the practices related to it we assume that we are free to do otherwise, and this assumption seems important to at least some of our judgements concerning that deliberation-based behaviour. And we would continue relying on this assumption *whether or not* our deliberation-based behaviours were considered things for which we could be morally responsible (Fischer 1989: 12).

1.2.2 Denying the Transfer Principle

Consider premise (3) from our argument for foreknowledge incompatibilism:

(3) If $N^S_t(p)$ and $N^S_t(p$ entails $q)$, then $N^S_t(q)$.

Premise (3) is a version of what is known as the *Transfer of Powerlessness Principle*. Such principles are used in arguments for the incompatibility of free will with causal or natural determinism, as well as arguments for foreknowledge incompatibilism. Their purpose is to formalise the following intuition: if someone has no control over one fact, and that fact entails a further fact and the person has no control over that entailment, the person has no control over the fact which is entailed. To illustrate, suppose that it's currently Tuesday and Andy has no choice about whether it's Tuesday. Its being Tuesday today entails that it will be Wednesday tomorrow, and Andy doesn't seem to have any control over that entailment either. But then it's intuitive to conclude that Andy has no choice about the fact that it will be Wednesday tomorrow (see Fischer 1989: 7 for further examples).

The argument for foreknowledge incompatibilism appeals to the same idea: Jones has no choice about whether God believed at t1 that she would decide at t3 to mow her lawn (after all, t1 could be a point in the distant past, e.g. 1 billion years ago); and she has no choice about the fact that God's past belief entails that she will indeed decide at t3 to mow her lawn (because she has no control over God's infallibility); therefore, Jones has no choice about how she ends up deciding at t3.

Given how intuitive such examples are, the rejection of the Transfer of Powerlessness Principle will seem "extremely puzzling", as William Hasker has said, unless one can go beyond pointing out that the examples don't prove the principle to provide some positive argument for its rejection (2001: 102). Some philosophers have indeed attempted to do this. One of the most influential attempts was made by Thomas McKay and David Johnson (1996), who challenged a transfer principle that Peter van Inwagen used in an argument for the incompatibility of free will and causal determinism. Despite their article generating significant discussion, scholars have raised problems for it. One is that McKay and Johnson's argument employs a strong interpretation of the 'N' operator which requires the agent to be able to *ensure* that a given outcome occurs. But, as Timothy O'Connor (1993) has pointed out, arguments for incompatibilism do not need to employ such a strong reading of the 'N' operator; they need only require that the agent be able to do something which *might* have a particular result. This provides one way to escape the McKay and Johnson objection. Another problem for McKay and Johnson's argument is that it targets a specific formulation of the Transfer Principle. As such, their objection might be conceived of as a 'technical response' inasmuch as it exploits a technical flaw in the argument's formalisation, rather than addressing the incompatibilists' underlying worry. And because of this, many philosophers do not consider it decisive since it looks as if the Transfer Principle can be repaired to avoid the objection they raise (see Speak 2011: 120 for details). For these reasons, denying the Transfer Principle has not been a popular response to the argument, and we say no more about it here.

1.2.3 Power over the Past I: Ockhamism

The next response we consider is called Ockhamism, named after the Franciscan friar William of Ockham (c.1285–1348). As we understand it, Ockhamism accepts that hard facts about the past – i.e. "over and done with" facts – are fixed and therefore outside of our control. What the Ockhamist maintains, however, is that facts about God's beliefs are soft facts about the past which are not fixed. The Ockhamist thus holds that the foreknowledge incompatibilist illegitimately applies the principle of the fixity of the past to facts about God's past beliefs (Fischer 1989: 33). According to the Ockhamist facts about God's past beliefs should be classified as soft facts akin to those examples introduced in Section 1.1:

> Uncontroversial soft facts about the past
> (1.2.3.1) Martin Luther posted his ninety-five theses to the door of the castle church of Wittenberg in 1517, 502 years before our publication of this Element (a soft fact relative to our time of writing in 2018).
> (1.2.3.2) Goran Ivanišević's 2001 Wimbledon win is the only winning of the men's Wimbledon title by a Croatian in the twenty-first century. (If this is a fact at all, it is a soft fact relative to our time of writing in 2018.)
> (1.2.3.3) Sally had toast for breakfast yesterday, forty-eight hours before she will have cereal for breakfast tomorrow.

If the Ockhamist is right about this classification of God's beliefs, then premise (2) of our argument

(2)　N^{Jones}_{t2}(God believed at t1 that Jones would decide at t3 to mow her lawn).

is false and the argument fails. After all, if facts about God's past beliefs are not fixed, then there is no fixity to transfer over to the future decision which God's past belief is about. The Ockhamist, in other words, affirms that facts about God's past beliefs concerning human decisions and actions are soft facts, and, moreover, that they are *non-fixed* soft facts. Affirming that facts about this class of God's past beliefs are non-fixed soft facts allows the Ockhamist to say, for example, that if Jones were to refrain from deciding to mow, God would have believed something different. And Jones's having this power would – so the thought goes – be no more problematic than Sally's having power over (1.2.3.3) (which she has in virtue of being able to refrain from cereal tomorrow) or our having power over (1.2.3.1) (which we have (at the time of writing) because we could delay the publication of this Element).

The main task for the Ockhamist is to justify the claim that facts about God's past beliefs are non-fixed soft facts about the past. This is difficult because, intuitively, facts about a person's past beliefs are hard facts about the past. Suppose that on Monday Kyle went to work wearing a black shirt. On Tuesday the facts about what Kyle wore on Monday are fixed. The same seems true of Kyle's beliefs: the beliefs that Kyle had on Monday were concrete mental states and, as a result, facts about them are, on Tuesday, as fixed as facts about what Kyle wore on Monday. Just as Kyle can't on Tuesday change the fact that he wore a black shirt on Monday, neither can he change the fact that he believed on Monday that the Greens would win an election in 2027.

In the recent literature on foreknowledge and free will, by which we mean the discussion that has taken place since Pike's 1965 paper 'Divine Omniscience and Voluntary Action', Ockhamists have pursued their project by attempting to provide a criterion which distinguishes between hard and soft facts and which classifies facts about God's past beliefs as non-fixed soft facts. The search for such a criterion was initiated by Marilyn McCord Adams. Adams began by defining the notion of a statement being 'about a time':

> (B) Statement p is at least in part about a time t = def the happening or not happening, actuality or nonactuality of something at t is a necessary condition of the truth of p. (1967: 493)

According to this definition the following soft fact (relative to our time of writing in 2018)

> (1.2.3.1) Martin Luther posted his ninety-five theses to the door of the castle church of Wittenberg in 1517, 502 years before our publication of this Element.

is (at least in part) about the year 1517 because the truth of (1.2.3.1) requires Luther's posting of his theses to the door of the castle church to occur in 1517. This fact is also, of course, partly about the year 2019 because that is 502 years after 1517. With definition (B) in hand, Adams defines the notion of a hard fact:

> (C) Statement p expresses a 'hard' fact about a time t = def p is not at least in part about any time future relative to t. (1967: 494)

What (C) says is that hard facts have no necessary conditions which must be met in the future relative to t. Together these definitions produce a version of what is known in the literature as an *entailment criterion* for soft facthood. The idea is that for any fact F which is in part about t1, where t1 is prior to the current time, if F entails a fact about some time t2 later than the present time, F is a soft fact.

How is this meant to help the Ockhamist? Well, given God's essential omniscience and infallibility, any fact about one of God's past beliefs about the future will come out as a soft fact. That's because God's infallibility ensures – and so entails – that what God believes about the future will come to pass. To illustrate, suppose it was a fact that in 1900 God believed that the Greens would win an election in 2027. Given God's infallibility, this fact entails that the Greens will win an election in 2027. Thus, that fact about one of God's past beliefs entails something about the future (relative to the writing of this Element) and so is a soft fact. It is a soft fact, moreover, at every time after 1900 and before the relevant election in 2027. But if facts about God's past beliefs are soft facts about the past, then we escape the argument for foreknowledge incompatibilism. That, at least, is the hope.

It was quickly recognised, however, that this simple entailment criterion of soft facthood is flawed because it has the result that all facts about the past are soft facts. Here is how Fischer makes the point:

> Consider the fact, "Jack is sitting at t1". This should be classified as a hard fact about t1. But notice that "Jack is sitting at t1" entails that it is not the case that Jack sits for the first time at t2 . . . Thus, [the entailment criterion of soft facthood] must classify "Jack is sitting at t1" as a soft fact about t1. Because this sort of result is clearly generalizable, it appears as if [the entailment criterion of soft facthood] will classify all facts as soft, and it is therefore evidently unacceptable. (1989: 35–6)

In the thirty years after the publication of Adams's paper, many attempts were made to develop an entailment-based criterion for soft facthood. This was often done by trying to isolate something that would guarantee hard facthood. Thus, Alfred Freddoso has appealed to the idea that hard facts are "atomic" facts that are "temporally indifferent" (1983: 145–56), Hasker that hard facts are "future indifferent" (1989: ch. 5), and Joshua Hoffman and Gary Rosenkrantz that hard facts are themselves "unrestrictedly repeatable" while not entailing any other facts that are "unrestrictedly repeatable" (1984).

The details of these – and other – proposals need not concern us, however, for three reasons.[4] First, suppose an Ockhamist presents an entailment-based criterion which (a) classifies all paradigm cases of hard and soft facts correctly (i.e. according to our intuitions), and (b) classifies facts about God's past beliefs concerning future events as soft facts. Would that suffice for a defence of the Ockhamist solution to the argument? There is good reason to think not. As any brief look at one of the extant criteria will make clear, they are very complex.

---

[4] We refer the reader to Fischer (1992: 98–100) for a useful overview of five major attempts to develop the hard/soft fact distinction.

And one worry that arises for any hard/soft fact distinction as complex as those found in the literature is that it has simply been tailored, in an ad hoc manner, to give the 'correct' – as judged by the Ockhamist – result. This is problematic inasmuch as any such criterion will, by classifying facts about God's past beliefs as soft, go against widely held intuitions concerning how facts about the beliefs of persons should be classified. Linda Zagzebski, herself a foreknowledge compatibilist, makes the point as follows:

> Most people have strong intuitions about the necessity of the past in a large variety of cases, . . . [and] the past beliefs of persons would automatically be put in this category [i.e. that of hard facts] if it were not for the foreknowledge dilemma. (1996: 75)

Zagzebski goes on to develop an analogy to illustrate the point. Suppose we were trying to articulate the distinction between just and unjust actions. Someone comes along who happens to owe Alvin Plantinga some money. This person proposes a criterion which classifies all the paradigm cases of just and unjust actions correctly, except that it classifies paying back debts to Plantinga as *unjust* actions. Various people note deficiencies in the proposal and offer repairs, the proposal is revised several times etc., all while consistently maintaining the classification of the repayment of debts to Plantinga as unjust actions. Zagzebski is surely right when she says that "we would think that something had gone wrong with such a definition" (1996: 75). We would think that the criterion was simply ad hoc: tailored to latch onto the just/unjust distinction except in a certain case which the author finds unsatisfactory (Zagzebski 1996: 74). This is the worry for any Ockhamist who puts forward a criterion for distinguishing between hard and soft facts which purports to show that facts about God's beliefs are soft facts. The criterion needs to have independent plausibility – and enough independent plausibility, moreover, to justify its acceptance even when it goes against our intuitions about paradigm cases (i.e. concerning the past beliefs of human persons).

The second reason for doubting that an entailment-based criterion which gave the 'correct' Ockhamist results would suffice for a convincing response to the argument is that it's unclear why we should think that *entailment* is the key to the distinction between hard and soft facts. Adams and those following her simply assumed that this was so, presumably because of an underlying assumption that if a fact entails something about the future, it is not "over and done with". But on closer inspection this might be doubted. As David Widerker asks, "what has a past fact's entailing a fact about the future got to do with its [not being fixed]?" (1990: 465). Why can't a fact that is fully "over and done with" entail something about the future? Entailing the occurrence of a distinct event doesn't seem to require that the thing doing the entailing isn't itself "over and done with".

Widerker has presented several examples designed to support this point and simultaneously to cast doubt on any entailment-based criterion of soft and hard facthood. Suppose, for one, that God *promises* Smith at t1 that he will find a marriage partner. And suppose that God makes this promise by speaking to Smith in an audible voice: this utterance constitutes a performative speech act that is God's promising. Such an event seems to be a paradigm case of something's being fixed: the utterance is locatable in time and space and has served as a cause for several effects (e.g. Smith's forming of various beliefs, a reduction in his anxiety etc.). Moreover, once the audible voice ceases, God's act of promising seems to be "over and done with". Yet God's promise to Smith *entails* that Smith will at some point in the future find a marriage partner (Widerker 1996: 98).

Third and finally, Hasker (1988) and Fischer (1986: 596–9) have contended that Ockhamism doesn't suffice as a response to the argument even given the assumption that there is an adequate criterion for distinguishing soft and hard facts which classifies facts about God's past beliefs as soft. Here we focus on Fischer's argument.[5] It relies on the observation that many soft facts about the past – including those about God's beliefs (if they are indeed soft) – are in some sense 'complex' facts. They are *in part* about the past and *in part* about the future (relative to today). One way of thinking about these facts is as being made up of various individuals possessing various properties. For example, the fact that God believed at time t1 that Jones would decide at t3 to mow her lawn is made up of God possessing at t1 the property of *believing that Jones will decide at t3 to mow her lawn* and Jones possessing at t3 the property of *deciding to mow*. Given this complexity in the relevant facts, Fischer points out that some soft facts involve the possession of what we might call a *hard property*. Hard properties – similar to hard facts – are properties that are "over and done with" at the time at which they are possessed. But hard properties, unlike hard facts, don't entail anything. *The fact that* God believed at time t1 that Jones would decide at t3 to mow her lawn *entails* that Jones decides at t3 to mow. But God's *having the property at t1* of believing that Jones will decide at t3 to mow is a property, not a fact, and so doesn't entail anything. Now, the problem for the Ockhamist is this. To falsify a soft fact about one of God's past beliefs requires doing something that would result in God's not having at t1 a hard property that He did in fact have at t1. But according to the Ockhamist our abilities to act are,

---

[5] In fact, Fischer has developed two such arguments, corresponding to two ways of dissecting 'complex' facts (see later in this Element). See Fischer (2016b) for more on this.

as Carl Ginet has said in another context, abilities to "add to *the given [hard] past*" (1990: 103) – the Ockhamist, remember, *agrees* that the hard past is fixed. That hard past includes *God's believing at t1 that Jones will decide at t3 to mow her lawn*, which is God's possessing a hard *property*, even if *the fact* about that belief is itself soft. Thus, if Jones has the power to refrain from deciding to mow her lawn, she has the power to do something such that God would no longer hold at t1 the belief that He does in fact hold at t1. This is a power which must be possessed and exercisable in the actual world *with its given past*. But, since t1 is in the past, this is impossible. Therefore, Jones cannot have the required power and so isn't free. The point can be put like this: it is not enough for the Ockhamist to show that facts about God's past beliefs are soft facts. The Ockhamist must also show that such facts aren't "hard-type soft facts" (Fischer 1986: 599), lest they turn out to be fixed nonetheless. This is no easy task, but without it, Ockhamism will be unsuccessful.

It is unsurprising, then, that, despite the popularity of the view in the years following Adams's presentation of it, discussion of Ockhamism died down in the 1990s. More recently, discussion of Ockhamism – or closely related views – has been revived. In this recent literature, much of the focus is on the nature of *metaphysical dependence* and whether that notion can illuminate the idea that God's past beliefs about future human free decisions are soft because they *depend on* those decisions. Trenton Merricks (2009) has presented one such solution based on a particular notion of dependence, and contended that it dissolves the problem. Fischer and Todd (2011) have replied to Merricks, suggesting that his solution fails to grapple with the fixity of the past. Other attempts at articulating a notion of dependence that would provide a response to the argument include Jonathan Westphal (2011) and Storrs McCall (2011). Fischer and Neal Tognazzini (2014) contend that these solutions too are merely the Ockhamist response couched in different terms, or else beg the question (i.e. presuppose the very freedom which the incompatibilists' argument is calling into question). Suffice to say that it remains to be seen how much of an advance the contemporary discussion, cast as it is in terms of dependence, will prove to be.

1.2.4 Power over the Past II: Multiple-(Hard?)Pasts Compatibilism

Hard facts about the past – those which are "over and done with" – appear to be fixed in the sense that they are now outside anyone's control. In this section, we consider responses which deny the fixity of the past.

We begin by looking at a version of this response put forward by George Mavrodes, one of the few philosophers to explicitly reject the fixity of the past.

His aim is to argue that "the past is not in general unpreventable" (1984: 139) and that therefore the argument for theological fatalism fails. Mavrodes uses a concrete example to illustrate what he means by preventable. Consider, he says, the reign of Elizabeth II which began in 1952 and is ongoing to this day. Mavrodes suggests that someone might have the power, now, to do something that would prevent Elizabeth II's reign. It's very important to understand what he *doesn't* mean here. Mavrodes is not merely saying that someone might do something now which would prevent Elizabeth II's reign from *continuing any longer*. (Someone might have such a power, of course, but that is not the relevant power.) Neither is he saying that someone might discover some technical error in (say) her coronation which would result in her queenship being declared invalid (1984: 139). What Mavrodes means by saying that Elizabeth II's reign might now be preventable is that "assuming that she has been Queen for many years, we might now be able to do something which would bring it about that she has never, up to the present time, been Queen" (1984: 139).

This is a bold claim, because Mavrodes seems to be saying that we might have the power to bring about some kind of alteration in the past. For the present purposes, however, what's important is to see how Mavrodes's claim purports to solve the problem. Mavrodes says that we might have a power to prevent Elizabeth II's queenship because the "pastness" of the past does nothing to put it outside of our control. He is careful to avoid committing himself to the idea that anyone does in fact have this particular power over the past (i.e. a power over Elizabeth II's queenship). Moreover, he remains open to the possibility that other features about the past – other than its *pastness* – may rule out anyone having power over it. His claim is just that the past *qua* past does nothing to put an event beyond our control. In other words, he flatly denies the fixity of the past. Given that denial, it might be that someone has the power to prevent Elizabeth II from ever having been queen. And what goes for the reigns of earthly sovereigns also goes for God's believings. This response to the argument functions, then, by denying premise (2):

(2) N^{Jones}_{t2}(God believed at t1 that Jones would decide at t3 to mow her lawn).

Premise (2) is denied, not because it is claimed that facts about God's past beliefs are non-fixed soft facts along the lines of the Ockhamist response considered in the previous section, but because it is claimed there is no such thing as the fixity of the past at all. As soon as that is denied, the argument collapses: if there is no fixity of the past, there is no fixity to transfer from God's past belief about Jones's decision to the decision itself.

It is at this point, however, that a problem begins to emerge. Recall that for Jones to be free with respect to her decision to mow, the following two statements must be true:

(1.2.4.1) Jones is able (just before t3) to decide to mow her lawn.
(1.2.4.2) Jones is able (just before t3) to decide to refrain from mowing her lawn.

Moreover, the sense of 'able' here must encompass Jones's possession of both the intrinsic ability to decide and the opportunity to do so. That is, Jones must be able to exercise her power to decide, and (just before t3) she must be able to exercise it either way. But that means it looks like the proponent of this response is forced to say that it is within Jones's power to prevent God from ever having believed that she would decide at t3 to mow her lawn, despite God's having always believed that very thing. And that looks very much like a power to change or alter the past (cf. Hasker 2001: 105). Consider that at t1 God believes something about how Jones is going to decide. We've supposed that Jones does decide to mow her lawn, so that's what God believes. Call God's belief that Jones will decide to mow her lawn *B*. That past belief, B, is part of the history of the actual world. If, just before t3, Jones really does have the power to decide not to mow her lawn – a power she possesses in the actual world, where God has belief B – then she has the power to make a certain decision which would result in God having had a different belief in the past. Whatever the precise nature of Jones's power to refrain, it must be that exercising that power would result in the actual world coming to have a different past than the one it does have. This must be the case because God is infallible: by hypothesis, if Jones were to decide not to mow her lawn, she wouldn't merely falsify one of God's beliefs.

Mavrodes defends this position by arguing for the coherence of what we might call *backwards bringing about*. Backwards bringing about is a relation between a source event which occurs at t2 and a result event which occurs at t1, where t2 is later than t1. When this relation obtains, the source event can be said to have *backwardsly brought about* the result event which occurred in the past. Mavrodes articulates such a relation because he accepts that it might be part of the conceptual content of our notion of *causation* that causes always precede their effects. If so, then backwards *causation* is conceptually impossible. But, Mavrodes says, that our concept of causation has this structure is no reason to think that there couldn't exist another relation very much like the causal relation which does not have such temporal constraints. And this is what Mavrodes refers to as the *bringing about* relation.

Mavrodes suggests that once this is accepted, the idea that someone might prevent something in the past from occurring is unproblematic. Jones's power to decide not to mow her lawn need not be a power to backwardsly *cause* God to have a different past belief. Jones's power 'just' needs to be a power to backwardsly *bring about* God's having a different past belief.

This position is very similar to that advocated by Alvin Plantinga (1986), in an influential – and ostensibly Ockhamist – response to the argument for foreknowledge incompatibilism. Plantinga, recognising the pitfalls in trying to articulate an entailment-based criterion of soft facthood, disconnects fixity from the idea of a hard "over and done with" past and defines it directly in terms of agential power (1986: 253). Whatever no one has an ability to do is deemed fixed.

Plantinga's treatment of Pike's version of the argument for foreknowledge incompatibilism might, at first glance, seem to be at odds with Mavrodes's response as outlined earlier in this Element. Plantinga is keen to distinguish between the following two abilities:

(1.2.4.3) Jones is able (just before t3) to bring it about that God holds a different belief from that which He does hold.
(1.2.4.4) Jones is able (just before t3) to do something which is such that, were she to do it, God would have held a different belief to that which He does hold.

Plantinga agrees that it is impossible for Jones to have the ability described in (1.2.4.3). But he maintains that Jones's possession of the ability described in (1.2.4.4) – which he calls a "counterfactual power over the past" – is possible and, moreover, unproblematic. The reason Plantinga eschews (1.2.4.3), however, seems to be that he reads 'bringing about' as causal, which is precisely what Mavrodes has denied (Mavrodes 1984: 142). Once we recognise that, we see the difference between these two positions is not as great as it might at first appear. This conclusion is bolstered when we recognise that on Plantinga's position it is possible for agents to have counterfactual power, not just over God's infallible past beliefs, but also over events such as Abraham's existence (Plantinga 1986: 253), the existence of past concrete occurrences such as the building of anthills in one's garden (Plantinga 1986: 258) and, we might add, Elizabeth II's queenship (and by extrapolation any other event or state in the past).

It is vital not to be misled by the labelling of this kind of power as "*counterfactual* power over the past". The adjective 'counterfactual' might suggest that the power is not real, or only possessed by Jones in some other possible world, or perhaps something else, any of which might suggest to Plantinga's readers that this kind of power couldn't possibly be problematic. This would be a mistake. The adjective 'counterfactual' merely refers to the connection posited between the action performed and the past event or state in question – in our case, the connection between Jones's (unexercised) power to refrain from mowing and God's believing at t1 that Jones will decide to refrain. Jones's power to decide to refrain from mowing must, it seems, be of the same kind as the power she does in fact exercise when she decides to mow. That's because, on the choice-based view of free will which we're working with, Jones's control comes from possessing and being able to exercise both powers. In other words, the powers comprising Jones's free will should be symmetrical in the following sense: in the concrete situation Jones is in, Jones has free will only if she possesses both powers, and both powers are exercisable, such that both unfoldings of the world – her deciding to mow, and her deciding not to mow – are genuine possibilities that Jones can realise. That is what it means to take seriously the idea that free will involves having a power to decide to mow and a power to decide to refrain from mowing and that each power is genuinely exercisable. But, the exercising of Jones's power to decide to refrain in her concrete choice situation would, according to Mavrodes and Plantinga, result in God's having had from all eternity a belief other than the one He does in fact have – i.e. would result in a different past – and, if it is accepted that Jones acts in a concrete situation *with a certain given past* (and what other situation could she act in?), this seems to amount to some kind of alteration in the past.

Following Fischer (1989: 53–5), we call this position *multiple-(hard?)pasts compatibilism*. On Plantinga's version of the view the hardness of the past is disconnected from its fixity, so it would seem accurate to call it *multiple-hard-pasts compatibilism*. On Mavrodes's version of the view the hardness of the past is jettisoned along with its fixity, so it might be more accurate to refer to it simply as *multiple-pasts compatibilism*. Either way, it differs from Ockhamism as we have characterised it because it does not seek to do justice to our intuitions concerning the fixity of the past and the asymmetry of the past and the future. (The Ockhamist, recall, denies that facts about God's beliefs are hard facts, but is keen to secure our intuitions concerning the hardness and fixity of other aspects of the past, such as Abraham's birth and Elizabeth II's coronation.)

The primary problem for this response is this very point: it doesn't do justice to our intuitions about the fixity of the past. If one denies that the past – the "over and done with", "fully accomplished", hard past – is fixed, then of course the argument fails. It fails because premise (2)

(2) N^{Jones}_{t2}(God believed at t1 that Jones would decide at t3 to mow her lawn).

is false. But what reason do we have for rejecting the fixity of the past? Of course, *if* we reject the fixity of the past, and endorse the view of power advocated by Mavrodes or Plantinga, then we can escape the argument, and we can do so without having to endorse any notion of backwards causation, and (for Plantinga) any notion of backwards bringing about. But we must still *reject the fixity of the past*. Yet providing an account of non-causal bringing about (Mavrodes) or "counterfactual power over the past" (Plantinga) does nothing to dull our intuitions that the past is indeed fixed. Endorsing those notions of power *requires us to reject* the fixity of the past but *doesn't provide a reason for doing so*. This is why Jonathan Kvanvig, for example, writes that:

> [It] would seem [that] Plantinga has missed the force of the argument which Pike and Aquinas have formulated [a version of the incompatibilist argument similar to that presented earlier]. For central to their formulations is the claim that the past is fixed in a certain way and is beyond the power of any agent to affect. Yet Plantinga gives no argument against this claim; his claims merely imply that it is false. (1986: 91)

We could put the point like this. The fixity of the past is, at least for many of us, one of those rock-bottom intuitions that would be incredibly hard, if not impossible, to deny. Indeed, this seems true even for Mavrodes, and perhaps for Plantinga too. Mavrodes, in a letter to Hasker, describes what it would be like to prevent Elizabeth II's queenship:

> Elizabeth has been queen of England for many years now. Suppose that I were to do something now whose effect would be that, while she has up to now been queen for many years, from now on she will never have been queen at all or at any time. I believe that it would be perfectly correct, and powerfully communicative, to say that by performing that act I had changed the past. (Mavrodes, as cited in Hasker 1989: 133)

Mavrodes then goes on to say,

> I really don't know how widespread [belief in the fixity of the past] is. But so far as I can tell, *I share it fully myself.* I have no inclination at all to think that I could perform any act which satisfied the description given above. (Mavrodes, as cited in Hasker 1989: 133, emphasis in Mavrodes's original communication)

So, intuitions concerning the fixity of the past are deep and widespread, apparently shared even by those who propose solutions which require denying such fixity. But – and this is the problem for the multiple-pasts compatibilist – having the power to delete from the history of the universe Elizabeth II's queenship (or God's prior belief that Jones will decide to mow her lawn, or whatever) and replace it with some other event is exactly the kind of power required by both the non-causal bringing about power that Mavrodes advocates and the "counterfactual power over the past" that Plantinga advocates. To the degree that one finds the fixity of the past plausible, then, one will find multiple-pasts compatibilism deficient.

1.2.5 The Atemporal Solution

In the presentation of the foregoing argument we assumed God is temporal. One way of resisting the argument is to deny this assumption and claim instead that God is *atemporal* or *timeless* and so does not believe things *at* times. For the atemporalist, the argument presented in Section 1 is evaded since premise (1) and all the premises which incorporate it are false.

On the atemporal view God's beliefs and knowledge are, just like God Himself, atemporal, and so God's believing and knowing are atemporal. God believes atemporally that Jones decides at t3 to mow her lawn. This belief is *about* a certain time, but God's act of believing doesn't itself occur *at* a time. Note that the content of God's belief must be understood as untensed: God's belief isn't about what Jones *will* do, but about what Jones *does at t3*. Being atemporal, God cannot have beliefs about tensed occurrences, because such beliefs would have to change. Boethius described God as believing and knowing everything "all at once" in an "eternal present" (1999: 134). The name "eternal present" is an attempt to describe the mode of God's existence. It borrows a temporal term, but it is not to be understood temporally. On one prominent understanding of the idea God's "eternal present" has no sequence of events or any duration.

Two analogies are commonly used to try to explain God's relationship to the temporal world. The first is that of the relationship of the centre of a circle to each point on its circumference. This analogy is obscure because it relies on the Neoplatonic idea that the centre of a circle is the *source* of each point on the circumference (Rogers 2007a: 8); just as the centre of the circle is the *source of* and so *present to* each point on the circle's circumference, so God is the *source of* and therefore *present to* each point in time, without Himself being in time or temporal. The second analogy asks us to picture someone on top of a mountain looking down on a road far below. Such a person can see the entire road 'all at once', whereas travellers walking along the road only see what is immediately in front of them. In a like manner is God meant to be related to temporal events: God is 'above' all time, not located in it, and as a result He can know what happens at each time.

The usefulness of these analogies may well be doubted. If nothing else, both rely on spatialising time, which is a highly controversial metaphysical move. In addition, the coherence of an atemporal agent has also been challenged.[6]

---

[6] For one such argument see Robert Coburn (1963); cf. discussion in Pike (1970: ch. 7).

Nevertheless, we proceed on the assumptions that an atemporal God is a coherent notion and that God tenselessly knows what happens at every time. The question is, do these assumptions generate a solution to the argument for foreknowledge incompatibilism?

Clearly, the atemporalist response successfully refutes the argument for foreknowledge incompatibilism *as stated earlier*. What's less clear is whether we have a decisive refutation of the underlying worry. The reason is as follows. Divine *fore*knowledge seems to threaten free will because, given God's infallibility, His past knowledge entails that the future decisions of all human agents are fixed before those decisions are made. But infallibility and *fore*knowledge are not the only things which result in such fixity. Infallibility and *timeless* knowledge appear to entail a similar sort of fixity, one that looks to be just as incompatible with free will. After all, in God's atemporal realm there is by definition no time and no change. Thus, if God believes *atemporally* that Jones decides at t3 to mow her lawn, that atemporal belief seems to be about as fixed as anything can be. This suggests that we can reframe the argument to rely, not on the fixity of the past, but on the fixity of the atemporal realm. This point has been frequently made in the literature, with Plantinga (1986: 239), Zagzebski (1996: 61–2; 2011: 72–6) and van Inwagen (2008: 218–20) all presenting versions of the argument for foreknowledge incompatibilism that apply when God is conceived of as atemporal.

The version of the argument we presented in Section 1.1 could be reformulated as follows:

(1') God believes tenselessly that Jones decides at t3 to mow her lawn.

(2') N^{Jones}_{t2}(God believes tenselessly that Jones decides at t3 to mow her lawn).

(3') If $N^S_t(p)$ and $N^S_t(p$ entails q), then $N^S_t(q)$.

(4') N^{Jones}_{t2}(God believes tenselessly that Jones decides at t3 to mow her lawn entails that Jones decides at t3 to mow her lawn).

(5') N^{Jones}_{t2}(Jones decides at t3 to mow her lawn).

(6') If N^{Jones}_{t2}(Jones decides at t3 to mow her lawn), then Jones cannot decide to refrain from mowing her lawn.

(7') If Jones cannot decide to refrain from mowing her lawn, she does not at t3 decide to mow her lawn freely.

(8') But, Jones decides at t3 to mow her lawn freely.

(9') Therefore (contrary to (1')), God did not believe tenselessly that Jones decides at t3 to mow her lawn.

The idea here should be clear enough. Instead of using the fixity of the past, the argument appeals to a kind of fixity which derives from the atemporal realm and aims to show that such fixity transfers over to a person's future decisions. This rules out the ability to do otherwise and so undermines the person's free will. We think this reformulation of the argument is itself very powerful and shows that the atemporalist response does not address the worry which motivates the incompatibilist. However, that is not to say this response is of no help at all to the foreknowledge compatibilist. Zagzebski has suggested that pre-theoretical intuitions about the atemporal realm and its fixity will, at least for some people, not be as clear or as strong as pre-theoretical intuitions about the past and its fixity (1996: 60). For such people, the atemporal version of the argument will not seem as threatening. And this means that the atemporal response to the original argument may well be a conceptual move forward, even if it is not by itself a complete response (Zagzebski 1996: 63).

How might one develop atemporalism into a full-blown response? Unsurprisingly given the structural similarities of the two versions of the argument, the atemporalist will need to combine atemporalism with another compatibilist response (e.g. Ockhamism, multiple-pasts compatibilism (which might become something like multiple-atemporal-realms compatibilism), or a denial of the Transfer Principle). Here we confine our comments to a single, recent presentation of a multiple-atemporal-realms compatibilism.

The account we have in mind comes from Katherin Rogers (2007a; 2007b). According to Rogers the conclusion of the argument presented earlier can be avoided because premise (2') is false. That is, God's atemporal beliefs are not fixed or necessary in any sense which would undermine the agent's control. The atemporal realm has only what is known as *consequent necessity*: given some event's occurrence, it is necessary that it occur then. But this kind of necessity doesn't undermine free will. God's atemporal knowledge doesn't cause the event's occurrence; rather, contingent events (including free decisions) cause God to atemporally believe what He does believe.[7] Rogers hopes to make plausible the idea that the atemporal realm is not fixed by appealing to the non-fixity of the temporal present. That is, Rogers suggests that, just as we can develop a version of the incompatibilist argument based on an atemporal God's beliefs, so we can develop a version of the incompatibilist argument based on a temporal God's knowledge of the present; and that there is a response to the latter argument (based on a temporal God's present knowledge of human action) shows that there is a response to the former argument (based on an atemporal God's tenseless knowledge) (Rogers 2007a: 17–18).

---

[7] It is difficult to explain how an atemporal God can atemporally know temporal events when it is agreed that the contents of God's knowledge are *caused by* those temporal events, as in Rogers's account (Rogers 2007a: 18). We don't pursue this difficulty here.

So, consider the very moment – t3 – in which Jones freely decides to mow her lawn. According to temporalists God believes *at t3* – i.e. at the present moment – that Jones freely decides to mow her lawn. But, Rogers asks, doesn't God's *present* belief produce a similar kind of fixity or necessity to that produced by any of God's *past* beliefs? She thinks it does. But if so, why don't the temporalist incompatibilists consider God's present beliefs to be a problem? They appear not to: temporalist incompatibilists affirm God has present knowledge of Jones's free decision while also holding that Jones is free. Thus, any fixity or necessity arising from the present cannot be threatening to free will. And if the determinate existence of God's present beliefs about our decisions doesn't undermine free will, we have little reason to think that the determinate existence of God's *atemporal* beliefs about those decisions undermines free will. Rogers, in other words, denies that the atemporal realm is fixed *in a sense which undermines free will*. Were Jones to exercise her ability to refrain from deciding to mow her lawn, the result would be that God would have atemporally believed a different thing about Jones's behaviour; Jones, then, has power over God's atemporal beliefs. And this seems to warrant classifying this response as a multiple-atemporal-realms response.

It is beyond the scope of this work to offer a full assessment of Rogers's response. One rejoinder to Rogers is to suggest that the necessity of the present *does* undermine free will. We have outlined Rogers's position here, however, not to critique it but to provide an example of a well-developed atemporalist solution which clearly – if not explicitly – recognises that atemporalism in and of itself does not solve the problem. What does the work is the denial that the atemporal realm is fixed. And it is this claim, and the arguments supporting it, that will likely be challenged. Interested readers are referred to Daniel Johnson (2009) and Hasker (2011), both of whom have argued that the present *is* fixed or necessary. If they are right, Rogers's attempt to defuse worries about the fixity of the atemporal realm by drawing a parallel to the present will fail.

1.2.6 The Open Future Response

Each of the responses considered so far has been a *compatibilist* response. There are also *incompatibilist* responses, which accept the validity of the argument and so hold that human freedom is incompatible with God's foreknowledge of future decisions. They thus reject either human freedom or God's foreknowledge. Rejecting human free will has not been a popular way of dealing with the argument and we won't consider it here, though the interested reader is referred to the work of Derk Pereboom (2009; 2016), a contemporary theist and free will sceptic. Rejecting God's knowledge of future human decisions, by contrast, is a position which has an increasing number of defenders. This position is known as the *open future response* or *open theism*.

Open theism responds to the argument by denying premise (1). It's clear that as a response to the argument, the position is impeccable. The issue for the open theist is that denying premise (1) brings with it its own set of (fairly big) problems. In this section we consider one purported theological cost associated with the denial of premise (1), namely, that it means denying God's omniscience (and so also God's perfection). Some authors consider it to be straightforward that God's omniscience must include knowledge of future free decisions of all His creatures. The following statement from Arthur W. Pink, in which he's commenting on God's knowledge of how Adam would behave in the Garden, is typical of many theologians' views on the matter:

> From God's standpoint the result of Adam's probation was not left in uncertainty. Before He formed him out of the dust of the ground and breathed into his nostrils the breath of life, God knew exactly how the appointed test would terminate. With this statement every Christian reader must be in accord, for, *to deny God's foreknowledge is to deny His omniscience*, and this is to repudiate one of the fundamental attributes of Deity. (1949: 176, emphasis added)

Many contemporary philosophers of religion also hold this view, as evidenced by this passage from Zagzebski:

> [T]he problem of divine foreknowledge arises from an alleged clash between two beliefs. The first is that God has infallibly true beliefs about everything that will happen in the future. This belief is grounded in the conviction that God is essentially omniscient. (1996: 4)

Writers such as Pink and Zagzebski think it follows simply by definition that God's omniscience requires that He knows everything that will happen in the future, and that divine omniscience is a non-negotiable feature of traditional theism.

In response to the aforementioned charge, open theists frequently raise the question of how omniscience should be defined, aiming to highlight a parallel with definitions of omnipotence. The starting point for an understanding of omnipotence might be the thought that *God can do anything*. But almost all Christian theologians will qualify this rather quickly. At the very least, there are grammatical sentences which seem to describe things that, on reflection, turn out to be logically impossible: e.g. the creation of a round square. The creation of a round square shouldn't be included in the 'anything' God can do because creating such a thing is impossible. Similarly, bringing it about that $2 + 2 = 5$

seems to involve the kind of contradiction that puts it beyond the realm of things that God can do. For this reason, the first step in defining omnipotence is to replace the 'anything' in 'God can do anything' with 'anything that it is logically possible to do' – a move that has been widely accepted at least since Aquinas (Hoffman & Rosenkrantz 2002: 167).[8]

According to some, though, this is only the tip of the iceberg of needed qualifications. Here is a list of things that one might think God cannot do: perform an evil action, perform a bodily action, cause Himself not to exist, bring it about (now) that a past event which has already occurred never did occur, and bring it about that a created agent freely decide to A (where A is some specified option). The crucial point about these types of action is that a reason can be given for thinking that God's not being able to do these things does not diminish His power: each is in some sense impossible for an omnipotent, immaterial being to do. If this is right, then it is legitimate to qualify the definition of omnipotence so that it does not require the power to perform these actions. But such qualifications do not mean it isn't really omnipotence.

Many open theists suggest that, just as the understanding of omnipotence must be nuanced to avoid incoherence, so the naïve understanding of omniscience needs to be qualified to avoid incoherence, and such a qualification is by no means a diminution of God's omniscience (Boyd 2001c: 41–3). Indeed, many theologians and philosophers who do not endorse the open future view make a similar point. That is, many theologians and philosophers – even aside from the issue of foreknowledge – accept that omniscience cannot simply be understood as 'God knows all things.' To begin with, note that omniscience is usually framed in terms of *propositional knowledge* (Zagzebski 1996: 4; Hoffman & Rosenkrantz 2002: 111; Wierenga 2017: sect. 1–2). If, therefore, other kinds of knowledge – such as *knowledge how*, or *knowledge of persons* – are irreducible to propositional knowledge, these other kinds of knowledge are not standardly taken to be required by omniscience. And in at least some cases one might think this restriction is both innocuous and desirable. Mavrodes, for instance, suggests that there would be something strange in requiring that the immaterial Creator of the universe know how to ride a bicycle (Mavrodes 2010: 252).

Even restricting our view to propositional knowledge, some have argued that we need to nuance the definition of omniscience. For example, it has been suggested that some propositions can only be expressed using

---

[8] Contemporary treatments tend not to talk of God's *performing types of action* but God's *bringing about states of affairs*; as our focus isn't omnipotence itself, we ignore this complication in what follows.

indexicals such as the first-person pronoun 'I' (see Swinburne 2016: 175–81 for a summary). Suppose Jones is in the hospital and thinks to himself, "I am in the hospital." He must – so the thought goes – know something different from an observer who utters "Jones is in the hospital," because if Jones were, say, suffering from amnesia, he might not know "Jones is in the hospital" is true, yet he might still know that "I am in the hospital" is true. This suggests that there are indexical propositions which can only be known by the speaker, which implies that there are true indexical propositions that God cannot know. There are ways of resisting this thought, and ways of working around it. Richard Swinburne suggests, for example, that what the aforementioned reasoning shows is that the correct way to think about omniscience is not in terms of *knowing all true propositions*, but in terms of *knowing of all true propositions that they are true* (2016: 177).

Our point here is not that Swinburne's way of addressing this difficulty is correct; rather, it is that indexical propositions provide a reason (and there may well be others), aside from any issues to do with foreknowledge, for thinking that the definition of omniscience will need to be qualified in some way. Now, open theists simply maintain that they too are adding a needed amendment to the definition of omniscience. Omniscience, they suggest, shouldn't be understood as requiring knowledge of how free agents decide in the future because such a thing is logically impossible. This response is developed in two standard ways. According to the first, endorsed by Gregory Boyd (2001c: 13, 42) and John Sanders (2007: 205) among others, the future does not yet exist and so there are literally no truths about future free decisions to know. Strictly speaking, open theists who pursue this route aren't qualifying the definition of omniscience, but are challenging the idea that the future is there to know – God knows everything about reality there is to know, it's just that everything there is to know about reality doesn't include facts about the future. The second way of developing this response accepts that there *are* truths about the future decisions of free agents but maintains that if any being were to know them, the decisions in question would no longer be free. According to this view, which is held by Swinburne (2016: 194–6) and Hasker (1989: 187ff.), omniscience must be qualified to include only that which it is possible to know. Either way, it is logically impossible for anyone – including God – to know how a created agent will freely decide in the future. And therefore, God's not knowing these things shouldn't be thought of as problematic. This claim can be challenged, but the likelihood that the definition of omniscience will require some qualifying aside from issues of foreknowledge shows that the open theist stance here cannot be easily dismissed.

1.2.7 Middle Knowledge

As we use the term, *Molinism* is the name of a doctrine of providence defended by Luis de Molina in the sixteenth century which relies on the distinctive idea of *middle knowledge*. Middle knowledge is one kind of knowledge possessed by God that purports to explain how God comes to have foreknowledge, or better, knowledge of what is future. It is called *middle* knowledge because it is said to lie 'in between' God's *natural* knowledge and God's *free* knowledge. God's natural knowledge is His knowledge of all necessary truths. This knowledge does not depend on what God wills. God's middle knowledge is His knowledge of contingent truths which do not depend on what He wills. God's free knowledge, by contrast, is His knowledge of those contingent truths which do depend on what He wills.

What kind of things does God know via His middle knowledge? The most important objects of middle knowledge are known as *conditionals* or *counterfactuals of creaturely freedom*. These are the propositions describing what each person – actual or possible – would do with respect to every decision he or she might face (or might have faced) and every action he or she might have (or have had) an opportunity to perform. They are expressed by sentences of the form:

> (1.2.7.1) If you were to go to Mildreds in Soho tonight, you would (freely) decide to have the katsu curry.
>
> (1.2.7.2) If Sally were to visit a pet shop on January 3, she would (freely) buy an iguana.
>
> (1.2.7.3) If Alex, whom God did not in fact create, had been created and the match on Saturday were cancelled, Alex would mow his lawn.

Several things should be noted. First, counterfactuals of creaturely freedom (CCFs) are, of course, about what people decide to do freely. We've highlighted this with the use of the 'freely' qualifier, but it shouldn't be thought that the use of the 'freely' qualifier settles any of the metaphysical objections to middle knowledge. Second, it is widely agreed that the circumstances described in the antecedent of the counterfactual need to be *maximally specified circumstances* (see Freddoso 1988: 50; Craig 1987: 138, 140; Flint 2011: 276–7; Hasker 1989: 32–5). Thus, the sentences listed earlier are only approximations of the counterfactual propositions which God uses to guide His decisions. And of course, it would be impossible to write out a maximally specified counterfactual descriptively. This is why the literature on middle knowledge often uses the following sentence form (where 'C' is understood as a placeholder for or the name of a maximally specified set of circumstances):

> (1.2.7.4) If Bob were in circumstances *C*, Bob would decide to eat a biscuit.

Middle knowledge is not exhausted by counterfactuals of creaturely freedom. It is supposed to include counterfactuals describing what would happen in any indeterministic situation. Some Molinists also endorse the view that there are counterfactuals of *divine* freedom describing what God would do in any situation. These purported objects of middle knowledge do not concern us here.

Middle knowledge is said to explain foreknowledge in the following way. Prior to creation – and, as most Molinists take God to be atemporal, this 'prior' is usually understood as indicating a 'logical' rather than a temporal moment – God knows all necessary truths and CCFs as well as counterfactuals of all other indeterministic events. God uses His natural knowledge and His middle knowledge to decide which world to create. Once God has made this decision and issued His creative decree, He then has free knowledge, which includes foreknowledge, i.e. knowledge of everything that will come to pass.

Middle knowledge, then, seems to provide a way to *explain* God's foreknowledge: it helps us to see how the different kinds of knowledge God has fit together. The question, however, is not whether Molinism *explains how God comes to have foreknowledge*, but whether the theory of middle knowledge *reconciles God's foreknowledge with human free will*. Some prominent Molinists certainly think so. Thomas Flint asserts that:

> The problems of foreknowledge and sovereignty are solved on [the Molinist] picture due to the fact that God's foreknowledge of contingent events flows from a combination of knowledge beyond his control and decisions under his control. (1998: 44)

We think not, however. To begin to see why, note the following. Divine foreknowledge is knowledge of what will in fact occur. On the presentist view of time, according to which only the present exists, foreknowledge is knowledge of what will be (but is not yet) actual. On the four-dimensionalist view of time foreknowledge is knowledge of what is actual, just not past or present. Either way, foreknowledge has a temporal connection to actuality. Middle knowledge does not: it is knowledge of a certain kind of possibility, and so the objects of middle knowledge have a merely modal connection to actuality. Why is this important? Well, it seems plausible to suppose that, *if* foreknowledge is (at the very least) a prima facie threat to free will because it seems to settle the outcome of a decision before it is made, *then* middle knowledge will also be (at the very least) a prima facie threat to free will because it too seems to settle the outcome of the decision before it is made, and it does so on the basis of a more 'tenuous' connection to actuality.

Our point here is not that middle knowledge is straight-off incompatible with free will; it is, rather, that one might think middle knowledge creates more of a problem for human free will than mere foreknowledge. Foreknowledge suggests that human decisions *in the realm of the future* are fixed or settled; middle knowledge suggests that human decisions *in the realm of the merely possible* are fixed or settled. Anyone who deems the former issue a problem worth addressing should, we think, also deem the latter a problem worth addressing. Yes, *given* middle knowledge, we can explain *how* God comes to have the foreknowledge He does in fact have. And so, as Hasker says, the theory of middle knowledge might strengthen any foreknowledge compatibilist position (1989: 18–19). Nevertheless, from the get-go there is reason to doubt that middle knowledge could provide a reconciliation of foreknowledge and free will.

We have already seen that Plantinga, who employed the concept of middle knowledge in his development of the free will defence, solves the problem of divine foreknowledge by denying that the hard past is out of our control (see Section 1.2.4). William Lane Craig, another prominent Molinist, endorses the idea that we have counterfactual power over the past, and writes that extant incompatibilist appeals to fixity-of-the-past principles are not yet developed enough to generate a troubling argument (1987: 80–1). This suggests that he too would question the fixity of the (intuitively hard) past. And Zagzebski (1996: 131–3) has detailed how Molina himself escaped the foreknowledge problem by denying the Transfer of Powerlessness Principle – i.e. by embracing the solution discussed in Section 1.2.2, thereby implicitly conceding that middle knowledge itself isn't a solution. This is also the route that Freddoso (1988: 58) seems to favour. The key point is that these replies are independent of Molinism: each can be advocated without endorsing Molinism, and Molinism adds nothing to them. We submit that the fact that many leading Molinists – including Molina – endorse one of the other compatibilist solutions given earlier is further evidence that the doctrine of middle knowledge is not in and of itself a solution to the problem of divine foreknowledge and human free will.

2 Divine Providence and Human Freedom

2.1 What Is Divine Providence?

In Section 1 we considered a possible threat to human freedom arising from a particular attribute of God: His knowledge. This is not the only attribute of God that relates to, and raises questions about, the nature and extent of human freedom. For God is traditionally conceived as not only a *knower*, but also as a *doer*. Unlike the deist idea that God created the world and then left it to function on its own, traditional theism has insisted that God continuously preserves the world in existence and guides the unfolding of events according to a plan that reflects His wisdom and power – from preparing the rain, making the grass grow and giving the animals their food (Psalm 147), to numbering the hairs on our heads (Luke 12:7), satisfying our needs (Philippians 4:19) and instituting governing authorities (Romans 13:1). God's governing the course of history is referred to as *divine providence*. But to the extent that God governs the world according to His plans, how much 'space' is there for humans to exercise their own free will? This is the question traditionally discussed under the heading of 'divine providence and human freedom'.

In what follows, we consider several different conceptions of providence and their related conceptions of human freedom. We begin (in Section 2.2) by looking at thinkers who have suggested that human freedom is *compatible* with God's determining every human decision but *incompatible* with natural, causal determinism. We deem this view unstable because the considerations which motivate incompatibilism in the natural, causal case also motivate incompatibilism in the theological case. It is not possible, then, to hold what might be called the 'strongest' view of divine providence *and* the 'strongest' view of free will; one of these views must be rejected.

The rejection of the view that God determines all things is motivated to a significant extent by concerns about the problem of evil, and so we turn next (in Section 2.3) to a brief discussion of this problem and how an appeal to human freedom has historically figured in a response. We then look at two views of providence – open theism (in Section 2.4) and Molinism (in Section 2.5) – which agree that God does not determine all things but diverge in their conceptions of God's knowledge. As we see in what follows, these distinct conceptions have implications for the level of risk God takes in creating free creatures and the responsibility He shoulders for the evil that such creatures commit.

Finally (in Section 2.6) we consider the position of those who affirm that God determines all things and maintain that free will is compatible with such divine determination as well as with natural, causal determinism. Since, as we note earlier (in Section 2.3), the appeal to human freedom made in response to the problem of evil seems to assume that human freedom is *not* compatible with God's determination of human action, this section focuses on how those who affirm God's determination of all things explain the existence of evil. We conclude this section by considering one argument against the view that God's determination of human action is compatible with human freedom, regarding the appropriateness of God's blaming creatures He has determined to sin.

Our aim in this section is not to defend any particular view of providence wholesale, but to point out certain 'costs and benefits' of each. As we seek to show, there is a kind of trade-off between divine and human control. To the extent that a view affirms God's sovereignty over creation, to that extent God seems associated with the evil that creatures do; but the more a view insists on human – and not divine – responsibility for evil, the more risk there appears to be in God's choice to create, and the harder it seems to affirm divine sovereignty.

2.2 Theological Compatibilism and Natural *In*compatibilism?

Theological determinism is the view that God determines everything that occurs in the world, including every human "thought, word, deed, desire, and choice" (Crabtree 2004: 7). On this view God hasn't just 'numbered' the hairs on our heads in the sense of having counted them; rather, He has 'numbered' them in the sense of having decided or settled precisely how many hairs are on our heads. And just as He settles how many hairs are on our heads, so He settles exactly which thoughts pass through our minds, which emotions we feel and to what degree, what we judge to be right and wrong, and exactly what we decide and do.

Most theological determinists, at least in the Christian tradition, affirm the existence of free will. This is because human responsibility for sin, and so the freedom that responsibility depends on, are central tenets of the Christian faith. All theological determinists who affirm the existence of human freedom are thus committed to compatibilism: the idea that human freedom is *compatible* with God's determining activity. We call such thinkers *theological compatibilists*.

Theological determinism (and the corresponding compatibilism) must be distinguished from *natural* or *causal* determinism (and its corresponding compatibilism). We follow Peter van Inwagen in understanding causal determinism as the thesis that "the past and the laws of nature together determine a unique future" (1989: 400). In the contemporary literature on free will this thesis is standardly referred to as *causal determinism*, but because some theological determinists conceive of God's determining activity as causal in character, we refer to it as *natural determinism*. Employing that definition, we say that *natural compatibilism* is the thesis that natural determinism is compatible with free will.

Many who have considered the question of whether free will is compatible with natural determinism – including many theists – conclude that natural compatibilism is false. That's because natural determinism entails that there are factors over which we have no control, which cause us to decide and act as we do; but then, we would not seem to have control over these decisions and actions either. This raises the question of whether one might be a natural *incompatibilist*, but a theological *compatibilist*. Of course, in one sense the answer is a straightforward yes. One can simply *define* these terms so that theological compatibilism and natural incompatibilism are consistent. The question is best understood, then, as asking whether such a position is plausible. And the answer to this seems to be a straightforward no. After all, if the reason natural determinism seems to undermine free will is that it entails that there are factors over which a person has no control which cause the person's decisions and actions, the same may be said of theological determinism: God's determining someone to decide seems just as much outside the person's control, and therefore looks to equally undermine human freedom.

Yet some philosophers and theologians endorse natural *incompatibilism* and theological *compatibilism*, and do not find the reasoning just presented compelling, instead maintaining that God's determining activity doesn't undermine human freedom as natural determinism does. Some, such as Kathryn Tanner, suggest that God's activity operates on a "different plane or axis" than that of human agency, so there is simply no conflict (1994: 118). Others endorse a doctrine of analogy, whereby they understand phrases such as 'bringing about', 'causing', 'settling', 'determining' and so on as taking on a different but related meaning when describing God's activity.

Now, we agree with Brian Shanley, one proponent of this sort of view, when he writes that "the limitations of human thought in the face of divine transcendence" must be acknowledged (1998: 116). Still, it is not enough to simply *say* that divine and human activity do not compete because they are on "different axes", or to *say* that God's determining something is only analogous to the way a creature might determine something. If God's determination is analogous to natural determination, they must have some features in common – otherwise 'determine' wouldn't be used analogically but equivocally, and that would simply be a change of subject. Since human freedom is prima facie threatened by divine determinism, proponents of theological compatibilism must either give some account of why there is in fact no competition between divine and human activity, or explain why it is not possible to give such an account.

When presenting their accounts, theological determinists use a wide variety of terms to describe God's activity. John A. Crabtree is happy to say God *determines, causes* and *wills* everything that occurs (2004: 7), while W. Matthews Grant favours talk of God's "universal causality" (2010; 2016). Shanley, presenting an interpretation of Aquinas, writes of God's "all pervasive creative causation", but denies that this is "determinative", despite the fact that God's causation leaves nothing "indifferent" (i.e. indeterminate) (1998: 117).

We submit that what matters is not which particular word is employed or avoided in framing the account, but the underlying concept, and in particular the modal implications of God's activity. So whether one uses the term 'cause' but refuses the term 'determine', or uses 'determine' but refuses 'cause', if the concept employed has all the properties of being determinative, or causal, refusing to use the label solves nothing.

One writer who has tried to explain why divine and human activity do not compete in any way that threatens human freedom is Hugh McCann. In the remainder of this section we outline and assess his account, developed most recently in conjunction with Daniel Johnson. McCann and Johnson are clear that we must reject the mistaken assumption that "God's will operates in the same way natural causes do" (2017: 10) and the idea which follows from it, namely, that God's will competes with ours for control of events in the world. They endorse the idea that God's determining what occurs is causal in nature, but hold that God's causal activity is unique in several respects. And it is these unique aspects of God's causal activity which are supposed to defuse the problem. First, unlike natural causes, which act "upon" already existing persons, and so may do violence to them by forcing them to act in ways that go against their inclinations or will (McCann 1995: 592), God causes our decisions and actions by "the same act of His will" that is responsible for creating us (McCann 1995: 590). Second, unlike natural causes, which predate the events they bring about, "God's activity as creator does not antedate" anything we do, since "God is a timelessly eternal being" (McCann 1995: 591). Thus, it cannot be said, as it sometimes is regarding natural causal processes, that our divinely caused actions are *consequences of events in the remote past* (see van Inwagen 1983: 16). Finally, God's causation of our actions does not involve event causation, as if God issued a command, and the event of God's commanding caused the event of our acting (McCann & Johnson 2017). Such event causation would rob us of our autonomy, McCann and Johnson reason, since God's command would be an "independent determining condition" of our actions (2017: 28). Instead, God directly brings about our actions, so that "the first manifestation of his creative activity regarding our decisions and actions is nothing short of the acts themselves" (2017: 28). McCann and Johnson thus maintain that even though all our decisions and actions are determined by God's will, those decisions and actions could satisfy any condition that the natural incompatibilist cared to lay down.

Suppose we grant McCann and Johnson this characterisation of divine causation of human activity – as producing one's very being and one's activity in the self-same act, as atemporal and as not involving event causation. A critic of their proposed solution might question whether these aspects of divine activity are all unique – and whether they (independently or jointly) solve the problem. Take the first claim, that God does not act "upon" already existing creatures to make them do things, but "creates them *in* their doings" (McCann & Johnson 2017: 28). McCann at one point suggests that this is a necessary truth – that "God *cannot* create me with an indeterminate will" (1995: 586–7, emphasis added) – since, he thinks, God cannot be "responsible for my existence at every moment without being responsible also for my characteristics" (1995: 586).[9] McCann reasons that since, "short of God's action as creator, there is no me to do anything" (1995: 590), it is not meaningful to ask whether I would have done something different had God not caused me to do what I in fact did (as it might be meaningful to ask whether, for instance, I would have done something different had another creature not forced me to do what I did). Now, let's agree for sake of argument with the claim that God's creative causality does not "do violence" to us *by forcing us to act against our inclinations or will*. Nevertheless, it does not follow simply from this fact that our freedom is compatible with God's causation. After all, according to natural incompatibilists (and some natural compatibilists), not all *natural* causes that deprive us of our freedom do so by forcing us to act against our wills. Some move us to act, not by overpowering us, but by 'winning us over'. As Watson notes, in the case of addictive behaviour, "we are not so much overpowered by brute force as seduced" (2004a: 71). There are also causes of our actions – e.g. our genetic makeup, our childhood environment and the social conditioning that we are exposed to early in our lives – which have such a 'hand' in forming our personalities, inclinations and will that it is not clear who we would be without these factors, or whether it even makes sense to ask what we would do were we not influenced by them. Still, many worry that such natural causes undermine our freedom and responsibility. And a similar worry might arise for God if He is responsible for our inclinations and will. McCann and Johnson may be correct that God's creative causality is unique in bringing us into existence at the same time that it moves us to act, but the conclusions they draw from this do not follow.

Let us consider, then, the second feature of God's creative causality which McCann takes to be unique: its atemporality. Recall that McCann notes, on the assumption that God is atemporal, that God's causal activity does not predate anything we do, and so it cannot be said that if God determines our decisions and actions, they were 'set in stone' long before we were born. Even if we accept this atemporal view of God and the view of divine agency that comes with it, two points still count against the claim that God's atemporality prevents

---

[9] However, he seems to retract this claim later, writing, "Perhaps there is a possibility, remote as it may seem, that God as creator has no fully settled will regarding our decisions, and so leaves indeterminate the world He creates" (1995: 590). We do not see why such a possibility seems remote or epistemically unlikely.

His creative causality from undermining our freedom. The first is that McCann's "atemporalist response" to the problem of divine providence and human freedom is parallel to the atemporalist response to the problem of divine *foreknowledge* and human freedom, described in Section 1.2.5. And, as we noted there, this response does not solve the problem, since an argument for incompatibilism about foreknowledge and free will can be given in atemporalist terms, drawing on intuitions concerning the fixity of the atemporal realm.

Some are not moved by this objection to the atemporalist response, of course, maintaining that there is no problem since the eternal realm is similar to the present, not the past, and any necessity associated with the present is compatible with free will (Rogers 2007a). These thinkers will likely be unmoved by the parallel objection to McCann's atemporality response. But a second objection may be raised, drawing attention to the way in which a synchronic, non-causal relationship might also threaten human freedom. Suppose that I am not *causally* determined to act as I do, but am *constituted* by particles that have a kind of autonomy of movement, such that their movement is not determined by pre-vious events, but my physical behaviour is *synchronously* determined by their movement. In other words, there is 'bottom-up' determination of the movement of the particles by my behaviour; my behaviour depends on the movement of the particles, not vice versa. Even though the movement of the particles does not *predate* my behaviour, it still seems that the determination of my behaviour by the movement of the particles robs me of free will when that is understood as being incompatible with natural determinism. But this case is parallel to McCann's picture, according to which "all of our actions depend on God for their existence, not vice versa, so that the perfect good for which he creates the world counts as the full and final explanation for what we do" (2001: 112). On such a picture what we do would *not* – contra McCann – seem 'up to us', just as my behaviour would not seem up to me if it were determined by the movement of particles which provide the "full and final explanation" for what I do. Of course, according to McCann, God's determination of our actions is not *simultaneous* with those actions, since simultaneity is a property of time, and God's determination is atemporal. However, the point is that what is most problematic about causal determinism (according to incompatibilists) is not its temporal properties, but the fact that determination of an event by something out of my control puts that event's occurrence outside my control as well.

We move now to the third feature of God's creative causality which McCann and Johnson take to be unique. They write that:

> We are prone to think of [the relationship between God's creative will and the things he creates] as an event–causal relation, in which God issues a kind of

command, and the command in turn produces the mandated effect . . . And of course this sounds exactly like what Aquinas describes as the violent opera- tion of an external principle . . . Clearly, however, this scenario does not reflect the way Aquinas thinks creation works, and on that score there is reason to think Aquinas is right . . . Rather, we and all that we do have our being *in* God, and the first manifestation of his creative activity regarding our decisions and actions is nothing short of the acts themselves . . . Accordingly, I can still display libertarian freedom [i.e. freedom that is incompatible with natural determinism]. My decision is a spontaneous display of creaturely agency, free in the libertarian sense because it does not occur through event causality, and because in it I am fully and intentionally committed both to deciding and to deciding exactly as I do. There are no further legitimate requirements for libertarian freedom. (McCann & Johnson 2017: 27)

McCann and Johnson suggest in this passage that natural incompatibilists see *event causation* as a primary threat to free will. But this can't be what most incompatibilists are most worried about, as evidenced by the fact that many of them develop *event-causal* accounts of free will. On such accounts, as long as the events over which I have no control are only *non-deterministic* causes of my decisions and actions, I retain control over those decisions and actions. Admittedly, some natural incompatibilists *do* think that event causation is a threat; but this is either because they think a free action must be *entirely uncaused*, or because they think that a free action must be *caused only by the agent herself*. Now, when McCann and Johnson describe God's causal activity, they seem to have in mind a form of agent causation. And one might wonder whether their picture would be amenable at least to agent-causal incompatibi- lists. But it would not. On McCann and Johnson's view a created person's action is *not* caused only by the person herself; because it is determined to occur by *God's* causal activity, it is also caused by God. This picture would thus threaten human freedom on all three standard natural incompatibilist models (event- causal, non-causal and agent-causal), since it involves *deterministic causation by something other than the agent acting*.

God's causal activity may well be unique in several ways. But McCann and Johnson have given us no good reason to think that theological determinism wouldn't undermine human freedom, on the assumption that natural determina- tion would.

2.3 Providence, the Problem of Evil and the Appeal to Free Will

We have argued that the theistic view which maintains that human freedom is incompatible with natural determinism but compatible with theological determinism is unstable. This means theists face a choice when it comes to understanding the relationship between divine and human agency: they must reject either the 'strongest' view of providence, according to which God determines everything that occurs in the world, or the 'strongest' view of human freedom, which requires theological (as well as natural) indeterminism. In this section we explore one important reason many theists reject theological determinism. The reason has to do with the problem of evil, and the way appeals to human freedom have figured in proposed solutions to it.

The problem of evil as it has been historically formulated is generated by the traditional view of God as all-powerful and wholly good. If God is all-powerful, He would seem to be able to prevent any evil that He wants to prevent; and if He is wholly good, it would seem that He would want to prevent all evil. But then the existence of God should preclude the existence of evil – and yet much evil evidently exists. The existence of evil thus calls into question the existence of God, traditionally conceived.

Over the past sixty or so years the problem of evil has received much attention in the philosophical literature, due in no small part to John L. Mackie's influential 1955 article, 'Evil and Omnipotence'. Mackie's argument was intended to demonstrate the *logical incompatibility* of the existence of God and evil. Arguments of this form have come to be known as *logical arguments from evil*.[10] Many philosophers now think the logical problem is solvable, since it seems logically possible that an omnipotent, wholly good God would allow evil to occur for some reason, such as that allowing evil enables Him to bring about some greater good. In other words, these philosophers question whether it is a necessary truth that a wholly good God would prevent every evil.

It wasn't long, however, before philosophers such as William Rowe (1979; 1996) formulated what is now known as the *evidential argument from evil*. Such arguments aim to show either (a) that some proposition about evil which we know with certainty is true makes the existence of God unlikely, or (b) that some likely true proposition about evil is inconsistent with the existence of God. In the face of this sort of challenge it is not enough for the theist to establish the mere logical consistency of the existence of God and evil. Much more must be said. In particular, something must be said concerning the proposition about evil employed in the argument, and why this proposition – if true – need not count as evidence against the existence of God.

In the history of Christian responses to the problem of evil free will has often been appealed to as part of the solution – the solution, at least, to the problem of

---

[10] In fact, this is an inadequate characterisation of the logical problem of evil. As Daniel Howard-Snyder has explained, logical arguments from evil are better characterised as those which claim that the existence of God is logically incompatible with a *known fact* about evil (see Howard-Snyder (1996: xiv)). We ignore this complication as it doesn't affect what we say.

moral evil. This response assumes the functionalist definition of free will discussed in the Introduction, namely, that free will is the control required for moral responsibility. The idea is that without free will, a person cannot be a *moral* agent, and thus (depending on how one understands moral agency) cannot do the right thing, manifest goodwill, be morally virtuous or what have you. The idea has often been developed by connecting this functionalist definition with a substantive notion of freedom according to which one must face *moral choices*, conceived of as choices between morally good and bad options. According to such a view a person cannot have the capacity for moral agency without at least the possibility of committing moral evil.

But couldn't God give people the opportunity to commit evil while ensuring that they always do good, by determining their actions? If God could do so, then the actual existence of moral evil would remain unexplained. Thus, if human freedom is to explain the existence of moral evil in the way we have just outlined, it must *not* be possible for God to determine what a created person freely chooses. In other words, this appeal to free will in response to the problem of moral evil assumes theological incompatibilism.

In addition to this metaphysical assumption – that free will places restrictions on God's control, since it is not possible for God to determine free choices – appealing to free will to solve the problem of moral evil requires relying on an axiological assumption, or value claim. One value claim that has often been employed in the theological tradition is that the moral agency made possible by free will is itself a great good – something of enough value to outweigh the disvalue of the moral evil it makes possible. If this value claim – or another like it – is also granted, then there is a justifying reason for the existence of moral evil, thus undercutting the claim that the existence of moral evil is evidence against the existence of God.

Given the prominent place human freedom has had in the history of theological reflection on the problem of moral evil, it is clear that a large number of thinkers have found appealing some version of this response, which we call a free-will-based theodicy. We do not mean to suggest, however, that they have always explicitly acknowledged, or consistently maintained, the assumptions on which it depends. It does seem fair to say that a vast majority of contemporary philosophers who have reflected on the problem agree that, *if* free will is what restricts God's control and so explains the existence of moral evil, then theological incompatibilism must be true. There is widespread agreement on this point among theological compatibilists and theological incompatibilists alike, though in Section 2.6 we consider the view of one who dissents from this majority opinion.

There is less consensus about the plausibility of the various axiological assumptions on which a free-will-based theodicy might depend. With respect to many of the value claims appealed to – including the one mentioned earlier, regarding the value of moral agency – it seems that whether a person finds them plausible depends on one's wider theoretical commitments, especially the theological anthropology one endorses, and one's view of morality. Yet these issues – the metaphysical claim, the axiological claim and the wider theoretical commitments which influence intuitions about that axiological claim – have not always been clearly distinguished, in either historical or contemporary discussions of free-will-based theodicies.

Several recent writers – including Adams (2006), Kenneth Himma (2009), Laura Ekstrom (2016) and Pereboom (2016) – have put pressure on the different value judgements that a free-will-based theodicy might employ. Ekstrom, for example, writes that:

> In order for a story along the lines of the free will defense . . . to be plausible, free will would have to be judged to be of such high value that it is worth the cost: the sum of all the pain and suffering that we both cause and endure as perpetrators and victims, including assault, bigotry, betrayal, sexual violence, child molestation, hatred, brutality, murder, and genocide, as well as a distribution of resources that leaves millions of people starving and in need of safe water and medical care, and medical malpractice that kills some patients and leaves others in permanent pain . . .
>
> Notice that we are aware of much that this phrase, "all of the pain and suffering in the world," includes . . . But of course there is more pain and suffering with which we are not familiar and which we cannot conceive in a way that makes its power vivid for us. It seems to me that, as soon as we try, and begin to pile it on to the scales, our weighing device simply breaks under the strain of it all. In fact, even making such a list . . . might tend to trivialize or mask from our view the significance of each individual case, in a way that makes us fail to appreciate the enormity of the problem. (2016: 63, 77)

Ekstrom concludes that the free will appealed to in these explanations of moral evil is *"just not worth it"* (2016: 77).

We think Ekstrom's comments about the amount and kind of pain and suffering in the world caused by free will are a powerful reminder of the seriousness of the problem of moral evil, and a helpful corrective against the temptation to offer too 'easy' a solution. However, when considering the plausibility of appeals to free will in explanations of moral evil, an important point must be kept in mind: most of these appeals depend crucially on an assumption mentioned earlier, namely, that free will is necessary for moral responsibility, and so the moral goodness that depends on free agency. Once this assumption is recognised much that Ekstrom says about moral evil can be said about moral goodness as well, and one weighed down by the problem of evil may also need a reminder: there is much moral goodness in the world with which we are not familiar, and which we cannot conceive in a way that makes its power vivid for us; in fact, even making a list of categories of moral goodness might tend to trivialise or mask from our view the significance of each individual case.

There is much more to be said about these issues, but for our purposes it suffices to say, in summary, that human freedom has played a significant role, historically and in recent times, in understanding and explaining the existence of evil in a world created by an omnipotent, wholly good God. This role has implications for the 'divine providence and human freedom' question which is the focus of the rest of Section 2. We turn next (in Sections 2.4 and 2.5) to consider two views of providence that assume the theological incompatibilism which, as we have noted, seems essential to free-will-based theodicies.

2.4 Open Theism

The first conception of providence we consider which presupposes theological incompatibilism is open theism. As an established position or movement within the church, open theism is a relatively new phenomenon. Groups throughout Christian history have advocated one or more of the key ideas maintained by open theists – divine temporality, divine mutability, the denial of exhaustive foreknowledge – but prior to the twentieth century these groups tended to be short-lived. In modern times important precursors to open theism include the work of Lorenzo D. McCabe (1882) and Swinburne (1977). Richard Rice's work (1980; 1985) began to establish the position in the United States in the 1980s. Arguably the most influential presentation of the position to date has been the 1994 joint publication by Clark Pinnock, Rice, Sanders, Hasker and David Basinger entitled *The Openness of God*. In the book's concluding chapter Basinger characterises open theism as affirming the following points, among others (1994: 156):

1. God created the world and can "intervene unilaterally in earthly affairs".
2. God gave us freedom "over which he cannot exercise total control". In other words, God cannot control what we freely do.
3. God so values our freedom that "he does not normally override" it.
4. God "does not possess exhaustive knowledge" of how we will freely act.

While the second characteristic listed here is affirmed by both open theists and Molinists and distinguishes them from theological determinists, it is the fourth characteristic that distinguishes open theism from Molinism. According to open theists God knows everything it is possible for Him to know: everything about the past and present, as well as everything about the future that is already determined. But what God cannot know is anything about the future that has not yet been determined, including the free decisions of humans. (See Section 1.2.6 for more on the open theist rejection of divine foreknowledge.)

Open theists largely agree that their view of God and His relationship to creation is not "traditional", inasmuch as it has not been the dominant position in "most of Christian history" (Rice 1994: 11). For these writers, the dominance of the traditional view, which includes a commitment to theological determinism as a component, is due to "the coupling of biblical ideas about God with notions of the divine nature drawn from Greek thought" – a coupling which "helped Christianity evangelize pagan thought and culture" but which, with its commitment to theological determinism, "infected the Christian doctrine of God, making it ill" (Pinnock et al. 1994: 8–9). Thus Pinnock et al. defend open theism in the hopes of "bringing about a healthier doctrine of God" (1994: 9).

Since open theists hold that human freedom is incompatible with divine foreknowledge, and since with most other theists they hold that human freedom is necessary for our moral responsibility, much hangs on their denial of divine foreknowledge. But open theists assert not simply that their view is *required* to make sense of these central tenets of Christianity, but that the picture one gets by denying divine foreknowledge – in which humans play a significant role in shaping the world, and in which God is responsive to human initiative – is profoundly biblical, and appealing. Pinnock et al. write that:

> The Christian life involves a genuine interaction between God and human beings. We respond to God's gracious initiatives and God responds to our responses . . . Sometimes God alone decides how to accomplish [his] goals. On other occasions, God works with human decisions, adapting his own plans to fit the changing situation. God does not control everything that happens. Rather, he is open to receiving input from creatures. In loving dialogue, God invites us to participate with him to bring the future into being. (1994: 7)

According to open theists, on the theological determinist's picture, the biblical representation of a God who is open and responsive to His creatures, who grieves our sin, who is surprised at what people have done, and whose actions sometimes depend on human prayers "makes no sense", because on that view God always gets exactly what He wants and is not conditioned by any of His creatures (Sanders 2007: 224). Basinger, developing the point about prayer, writes that, in contrast to theological determinists, open theists can affirm that petitionary prayer sometimes "initiates unilateral divine activity that would not have occurred if we had not utilized our God-given power of choice to request such divine assistance" (1994: 160). On the theological determinist's view all human prayer is determined by God "from eternity", as it were. So while the theological determinist can affirm that God's response to a prayer would not have occurred if the prayer hadn't been made, and in this way that God's response *logically* depends on the prayer, there is a sense in which God's activity is not dependent on His creatures' activity. For the ultimate explanation of both the created person's prayer and God's response is, on the theological determinist's view, God's creative will. In contrast, on the open theist's view the ultimate explanation for the person's prayer is *not* God's will, and the ultimate explanation for God's response to the prayer must in part involve that prayer – so God's activity depends on the person's activity in this further explanatory sense.

The claim that free will, moral responsibility and relationality require the denial of divine foreknowledge has, of course, been challenged. Moreover, some of the consequences of open theism that its proponents uphold as attractive features of the view have been found by others to be rather disconcerting. For instance, in his discussion of the character of divine guidance, Basinger describes what he takes to be a "benefit in assuming that God does not have exhaustive knowledge of the future" (1994: 164). Imagine, he says, that a person asks God for guidance about what to study, and comes to the conclusion that God is guiding her into a particular field. But then suppose that at the end of her studies she cannot find any employment in that field. When analysing this situation, Basinger says, all Christians have a couple of options. We could say that the "person's own intense desire for the job was wrongly interpreted as God's will", or that while the person discerned God's will correctly, she was incorrect in judging the subsequent unemployment to be a bad thing – God must have had other purposes for guiding her to study the given subject (1994: 165). Basinger suggests, however, that open theists have a third option. They can maintain that "since God does not necessarily know exactly what will happen in the future, it is always possible that even that which God in his unparalleled wisdom believes to be the best course of action at any given time may not produce the anticipated results in the long run" (1994: 165). Basinger considers this to be a benefit of the open view, since an individual who continued to believe she had correctly discerned God's will despite the disappointing outcome would be "free to turn to God without remorse or guilt to attempt to discern his new specific will for her life" (1994: 166).

Bruce Ware, a prominent critic of open theism, maintains that on the open theist view it is always possible that "God got it wrong" (2001: 170). To illustrate Ware's point using Basinger's example, God might have advised the student to pursue a course of study on the belief that it would lead to the best outcome (i.e. result in a job), but then it might not result in the job (because of an unforeseen change in the economic situation, say), and so it might turn out not to have been the best outcome after all. Now, *if* the open theist is committed to holding that God could end up 'getting it wrong' or holding false beliefs, then open theism has a serious problem. God's holding false beliefs is something that no one who claims to be committed to God's cognitive perfection can tolerate.

Nevertheless, it's not clear that the open theist *is* committed to this consequence. For one thing, it's not obvious that someone who advises another to *X* must believe that *X*-ing will, whatever else occurs, result in the best outcome possible. Perhaps the person giving advice only need believe that the advised course of action will *probably* yield the best outcome. So one option is for the open theist to deny that God has beliefs about undetermined events of the form 'event E will certainly occur', maintaining instead that God only believes that undetermined events will occur with a certain probability.

Alternatively, the open theist could note that God's advice might have the following form: if you do this, *and assuming various other people play their parts*, then the best outcome will certainly come to pass. Or, the open theist might deny that God gives advice concerning such specifics at all! Of course, this last move would undercut the positive reason Basinger cites for open theism, and seems at odds with the biblical witness, so it is unlikely to be congenial to the open theist. Even so, the first two responses are enough to show that, contra Ware, the open theist doesn't have to hold that every belief of God's "that relates in the slightest to [future] free creaturely choices and actions" is potentially wrong (Ware 2001: 170).

However, the problem just discussed is symptomatic of potentially more difficult objections to open theism. The common core of these challenges stems from the *riskiness* of God's activity, which in turn arises from His lack of knowledge concerning undetermined future events – free human decisions and, perhaps, other indeterministic events (e.g. quantum indeterminacies; see Boyd 2001a: 109). Open theists themselves embrace the language of risk; they see it as an unavoidable consequence of the claim that God seeks to establish genuine relationships with created persons and afford them a role in shaping the world and their own moral characters. It has been alleged, though, that this riskiness would (a) undermine a "high view of divine revelation" (Helm 2004), (b) prevent God from being able to answer petitionary prayers (a charge closely related to the one discussed earlier, viz., God's potentially giving mistaken advice) (Ware 2001: 173–6), and (c) prevent God from achieving His salvific purposes. In what follows we focus on the last objection, and consider how the view of Boyd, an early advocate of open theism, fares against it.

Boyd maintains that his open theist view is able to "render intelligible God's ability to bring good out of evil and ultimately defeat evil and accomplish his overall purposes for creation" (2011: 187). Among God's central purposes for creation, Boyd identifies created persons' receiving and reflecting God's love. "Before the creation of the world, God predestined that he would acquire a people ... who would receive the Father's perfect love for the Son and participate in the Son's perfect love for the Father" (2011: 188).

However, since on Boyd's view love is a *moral virtue* (2011: 188), and according to open theists the formation of moral virtue is incompatible with theological determinism, it follows that if God determined our response to His love, our response could not itself be a *loving* one. As Boyd affirms, "If God wants ... a people who *genuinely* love him and each other, he must create us with the capacity to choose to love *or not*" (2011: 189). But that suggests that on an open theist view like Boyd's, God *cannot* guarantee that "[He] would acquire a people ... who would receive the Father's perfect love for the Son", because He cannot guarantee that created people will respond positively to His offer of salvation.

One line of reply to this challenge is to endorse a corporate view of election. Rice, for instance, asserts that the biblical concept of divine election "applies to groups rather than individuals", and cites "an extensive survey of references to election" by William Klein, who suggests that the "plural language" of the New Testament election texts creates "the overwhelming impression ... that God has chosen the church as a body rather than the specific individuals who populate that body" (Rice 1994: 57). Boyd, who shares this impression, attempts to use this point to address the objection. He offers an analogy: "From a quantum mechanical perspective, all regularity in the phenomenological world is *statistical*. This does not undermine the real stability of nature's regularity ... The nature of [quantum] particles is such that we can say how they are *in general* disposed to act ... but we cannot say exactly how any *particular* particle *will* in fact act" (2001b: 152). He continues, "we should in principle be no more confounded by the fact that God can guarantee certain outcomes without meticulously determining their means than we are at how we can rely on the stability of the desk in front of us even though it is composed of quantum particles that are to some extent unpredictable" (2001b: 153). Boyd maintains that while God cannot foreknow that any particular individual will freely choose to love Him, He can foreknow that "a certain percentage range of people" will (2001b: 156), since people are to such an extent predictable in the aggregate. He insists that God foreknew not with some *probability* that He would have "a people" in the end, but with absolute certainty: the "probability" of this happening, he says, was "100 percent" (2001b: 177).

The critic is unlikely to be satisfied with this response, however. After all, if it is possible for *any particular* individual to reject God's love, isn't it also possible for *all* individuals to do so? If so, then the probability that all humans will reject God cannot be zero. And that seems to be enough to establish that God can't *guarantee* Himself a people who respond to Him with love. Grössl and Vicens (2014) push this line of objection.

Open theists might simply accept the conclusion but argue that it is inconsequential. Hasker appears to adopt this kind of approach:

> [E]ven if it is possible, on the open view of God, for all human beings without exception to reject salvation, still this might be overwhelmingly improbable – so improbable that the risk of such an outcome is negligible. Consider a parallel: According to modern physics, there is a finite probability that all of the oxygen in a room should concentrate itself in a small volume, leaving the rest of the room devoid of oxygen and unable to sustain life. But the probability of this happening is so minute that rational persons can and do disregard the possibility in conducting their lives … So why should our inability to show how God can logically guarantee that humans will respond to his love constitute a serious objection? (1994: 153)

Hasker is effectively conceding the point, but suggesting that it doesn't constitute an objection to open theism – or at least, not a very strong one. Hasker's point might be bolstered as follows. While open theists value free will for a variety of reasons, they are not committed to any kind of 'Sartrean' view according to which free agents are always able to rise above any and all situational influences and make a radically free choice. Open theists can accept a view of free will on which the agent's inner psychological states and external circumstances condition free decisions to some degree – perhaps by raising or lowering the probability of those decisions. How does that help? Well, God might arrange circumstances for individuals to make it very likely that they'll come to faith freely. If God does this enough times, the probability of at least some people coming to faith will be extremely high, perhaps high enough to justify Hasker's claim that the probability of no one coming to faith is negligible.

2.5 Molinism

Molinism is the view that God has middle knowledge, i.e. knowledge of contingent truths which do not depend on what God wills. In the previous section we considered whether middle knowledge reconciles divine foreknowledge and human freedom. Here we look at how middle knowledge adds to God's providential control.

The most important objects of middle knowledge for our purposes are *counterfactuals of creaturely freedom* (CCFs), which, as mentioned in Section 1, have the following form:

If person P were placed into circumstances C, P would decide to X.

True CCFs both facilitate and constrain God's providential control. They constrain it because, if there are such truths, some possible scenarios cannot be realised by God. For instance, suppose the following is true:

(2.5.1) If Penelope were to visit Joe's Travel Agency at 10:00 AM on October 17, 3043 . . ., Penelope would decide to go to Lisbon.

According to the Molinist, if (2.5.1) is true, then God simply finds Himself faced with the truth of this proposition. The truth of (2.5.1) is contingent, yet not something God Himself settles. And if this CCF is true, God cannot create Penelope, put her in the circumstances described in the antecedent of the counterfactual and have her decide to go to Minsk. If God creates Penelope and puts her in the specified circumstances, she *will* decide to go to Lisbon. This point applies to all CCFs and, therefore, for any given universe containing free creatures that God might bring into existence, there are some unfoldings of that universe which God cannot realise or, in the contemporary jargon, *actualise*. The possible worlds which God cannot actualise are known as *infeasible* worlds; those He can actualise are called *feasible*.

Despite the restrictions on God's control just outlined, it should also be clear that God's knowledge of the set of true CCFs enhances God's providential control. For God's creative decree can be informed by which CCFs He knows to be true. If, for example, (2.5.1) is true, then God knows that He can get Penelope to decide to go to Lisbon by placing her in the situation where she visits Joe's Travel Agency at 10:00 AM on October 17, 3043. And if God similarly knows the truth value for every CCF pertaining to Penelope, and every CCF pertaining to each possible person, then God has an enormous amount of control over how things unfold. Moreover, Molinists typically hold that God could have chosen not to create anything at all, which further adds to God's control.

Proponents of Molinism are not shy in claiming that middle knowledge is the "most fruitful of theological concepts" (Craig 2001: 125) which provides a large array of benefits to the theorist who will get on board the Molinist train. Those who get on board are promised the reconciliation of a 'strong' doctrine of providence with a 'strong' account of free will, as well as accounts of prophecy, petitionary prayer, papal infallibility (Flint 1998: 180–96), biblical inspiration (Craig 1999) and salvific exclusivism (Craig 1989) which are supposed to show how God can ensure some outcome (such as the contents of a prophetic pronouncement, once made) that depend on free choices undetermined by God.

Inasmuch as Molinism yields a strong doctrine of providence compatible with creaturely activity undetermined by God, it is an attractive position. Nevertheless, it remains a controversial position facing numerous objections. These can be usefully categorised as follows: first, there are what we might call theoretical objections that challenge some part of the philosophical machinery required by middle knowledge; second, there are practical objections to some of the implications Molinism has for doctrine. The most prominent theoretical objection is known as the *grounding objection*. The objection begins with a question: what makes the true CCFs true? By hypothesis, it is not God; yet neither can it be the human agents the CCFs are about, since most of them never exist, and the true CCFs about those agents who will exist are true before God creates them. The true CCFs, then, seem quite mysterious: they are contingent, and yet nothing seems to make them true. Because the issues here quickly get technical, and seem to depend to a large extent on one's intuitions concerning whether truths in general need to be 'grounded', we say nothing more about this objection. Other theoretical objections include (a) the 'bringing about' argument, which suggests that if there are true CCFs and their truth is not settled by the agent who is the subject of the CCF, then the agent in question isn't able to decide otherwise and so isn't free (Hasker (1989; 1999); see Flint (1999) for a response), and (b) the charge that Molinism is parallel to causal compatibilism in a significant way, such that Molinists cannot consistently endorse the consequence argument for incompatibilism (Cohen 2014). We say nothing further about those issues, either. Instead, we assume that God has middle knowledge compatible with human freedom and proceed to assess some of the practical objections to Molinism. In particular, we focus on whether Molinism entails that God intends every instance of moral evil humans commit, and, relatedly, whether Molinism affects the kind of response to the problem of evil one can give.

Divine Intention of Moral Evil

If God has middle knowledge, then for any creative decree He might issue, God knows exactly what would come to pass because of that decree, including every aspect of each instance of evil. This is not surprising, of course. Molinists aim to secure a 'traditional' understanding of providence which Freddoso has described thus:

> God, the divine artisan, freely and knowingly plans, orders, and provides for all the effects that constitute His artefact, the created universe with its entire

history, and executes His chosen plan by playing an active causal role sufficient to ensure its exact realization . . . Thus, whatever occurs is properly said to be specifically decreed by God. (1988: 3)

While this level of control seems appealing when we focus on the *goods* that creation contains, things may look different when we consider that God's control pertains to the *evils* too. To clarify what the problem is, we introduce Alan Rhoda's definitions of 'strongly actualise' and 'weakly actualise':[11]

To 'strongly actualise' an event is to be an ultimate sufficient cause of it.

To 'weakly actualise' an event is to strongly actualise conditions knowing for certain that they will lead to the event, despite the fact that those conditions are not causally sufficient for it. (2010: 283)

Additionally, we follow Rhoda and say that to *ordain* an event is to either strongly or weakly actualise it (2010: 283).

Given these definitions, it should be uncontroversial that, on the Molinist picture, God ordains all events. This idea is evident in the quote from Freddoso, and it's clearly endorsed by Flint in his description of the "traditional picture" of providence – which he takes the Molinist to be defending – as one in which God "knowingly and lovingly directs each and every event involving each and every creature toward the ends he has ordained for them" (1998: 12). For the Molinist, then, God *at the very least* ordains each instance of evil.

Hasker (1992: 98–9) and Rhoda (2010: 294ff.) have both argued, however, that this ordaining of each evil amounts to God's specifically (and problematically) *intending* each evil. Their claim is not that this ordaining amounts to God's intending each evil *for its own sake*; nevertheless, it amounts to God's intending each evil as part of the "complete package" of the universe that God has chosen to actualise, and that is bad enough (Rhoda 2010: 295). Rhoda explains why he considers this a problem:

[Molinism has] God actualizing creatures knowing they are going to commit heinous sins . . . [But] instrumental justifications of moral evil are condemned in scripture, and while Molinism doesn't have God *doing* or *causing* moral evil for the sake of greater goods that will result, it does have God *ordaining* moral evil for the sake of greater goods that will result. This renders God a deliberate accessory to moral evil. (2010: 296)

Rhoda is clear that because Molinism has God ordaining each evil – meaning either that God is an ultimate sufficient cause of the evil or that He actualises conditions He knows will certainly lead to the evil – Molinism implies that God *specifically intends* each evil, at least as part of the complete package of the

---

[11] This distinction was initially articulated by Plantinga (1978: 173).

world that is actualised (2010: 295). This seems intuitively problematic, and, as Rhoda points out, reasons can be given to support this thought (e.g. that it amounts to an instrumental justification of evil).

One way Molinists have tried to blunt the force of this objection is by appealing to the distinction between positively willing something on the one hand, and *merely permitting or allowing* it on the other. God, in weakly actualising the Bosnian genocide, didn't positively will the genocide; rather, He merely allowed it. And this is supposed to enable us to say that, even if there is *a sense* in which God intended that genocide, it is only a weak sense of 'intend', very much unlike the sense in which those who perpetrated the genocide intended it. Developing this idea, Craig writes the following:

> Molina defines providence as God's ordering of things to their ends, either directly or mediately through secondary agents. Molina carefully distinguishes between God's absolute intentions and his conditional intentions concerning free creatures. It is, for example, God's absolute intention that no creature should ever sin and that all should reach heaven. But it is not within God's power to determine what decisions creatures would freely take in various circumstances. In certain circumstances, creatures will freely sin, despite the fact that it is God's will that they not sin. If, then, God for whatever reason wants to bring about those circumstances, he has no choice but to allow the creature to sin, even though that is not his absolute intention. God's absolute intentions are thus often frustrated by sinful creatures, but his conditional intentions, which take into account creatures' free actions, are always fulfilled ... God's providence, then, extends to everything that happens, but it does not follow that God wills positively everything that happens. God wills positively every good creaturely decision, but evil decisions he does not will but merely permits. (2017: 35)

In this passage Craig's aim seems to be to use the distinction between "absolute" and "conditional" intentions to justify the claim that while God's providence extends to all events, God doesn't "will positively" everything that happens. God's "absolute intentions" are frustrated by the evil done by humans; and for that reason we can affirm that God "wills positively" only the good. His "absolute intentions" are thus linked to God's "willing positively". God's "conditional intentions", by contrast, "take into account" what free creatures do, even if it is evil; these intentions facilitate God's meticulous control over everything, but, because these intentions are not God's "absolute intentions", we can justifiably claim that God doesn't "will positively" evil, but "merely permits" it.

In order to assess Craig's proposal, two things must be noted. First, the distinction between "absolute intentions" and "conditional intentions" is not a distinction between *intentions* as those are understood in contemporary philosophy of action. "Absolute intentions" as characterised here are a kind of desire. They are what an agent 'really wants', 'most wants' or 'would want in idealised conditions'. What God most wants is for His creatures to live sin free. But He can't have that, because the true CCFs make it impossible. Now, if one knows something to be impossible, then while one may be able to *desire* it, one cannot *intend* it. And for precisely this reason God doesn't "absolutely" *intend* that no creature ever sin – rather, He "absolutely" *desires* that no creature ever sin. God's "absolute" desire that no creature ever sin is akin to Percy's "absolute" desire that the sun not rise tomorrow. Both are impossible in the relevant sense: God can't actualise (create) an infeasible world; Percy can't actualise (bring about) a situation where the sun doesn't rise tomorrow.

Second, the "conditional intentions" are said to be "conditional" because "they take into account creatures' free actions", but intentions which are "conditional" in this sense are perfectly ordinary intentions. Whenever any agent forms an intention to do something, that agent does so against some set of background beliefs about how the world is and will be. Some of these background beliefs are about aspects of the world which make the action possible; others are about what other agents are doing or will be doing. Crucially, though, when such beliefs constitute *knowledge*, the intention formed isn't "conditional" in the sense of *depending on some condition that might as yet go unfulfilled*; rather, the intention formed is "conditional" merely in the sense of being an intention to act in some given context. All ordinary, everyday intentions are "conditional" in this latter sense. And, on the Molinist view, it is only in this latter sense of "conditional" that the intentions God forms that "take into account" how free creatures act are conditional.

We highlight these two points because it is intentions (the so-called conditional intentions described by Craig) rather than desires (Craig's "absolute intentions") that matter most when morally assessing an agent's action. Here's an illustration: suppose that Matt has some bad news to give to his boss, Jen, and he knows that she's skipped lunch today and that whenever she's given bad news after skipping lunch, she flies off the handle at the next person she sees. Now imagine that Matt also knows Jen has a meeting with Jeremy and, disliking Jeremy, Matt asks him to deliver the bad news report to Jen, whereupon Jen starts verbally abusing Jeremy. Matt's beliefs about how other agents would act formed part of the context of his action, and they contribute to the meaning and moral status of his action. Matt didn't simply *give Jeremy a report to give to Jen*; no, given his knowledge, *Matt's giving Jeremy the report for Jen* is describable as a case of *Matt's arranging for Jeremy to be verbally abused*. Matt *intended* for Jeremy to be verbally abused. Matt's intention here counts as a "conditional" intention on Craig's terms, because it "took into account" how other people would act. There is nothing mysterious about that because the "conditional" intentions described by Molina/Craig are just ordinary intentions. And, crucially, because Matt *intended* for Jeremy to be verbally abused, we can say that he *positively willed* this, and did not *merely permit* it.

More generally, it should be recognised that the distinction between "absolute intentions" and "conditional intentions" – more accurately, the distinction between ultimate desires and normal intentions – cannot be used to justify an appeal to the "positively wills"/ "merely permits" distinction. Craig wants to say that God doesn't "will positively" – or, as we might say, *intend* in any substantial sense – evil, but merely *permits* it. But, just as we would not say that Matt *merely permitted* Jeremy to be verbally abused by Jen, neither should we say that the Molinist God *merely permits* evil to occur. If this is still doubted, imagine Matt having the choice between giving Jen the bad news himself, passing the report to Jeremy to give to Jen, and buying Jen some lunch and giving her the report after she'd eaten it. If those were Matt's options, it is surely implausible to say that he *merely allowed* Jeremy to be verbally abused. And similarly, one might think, given that God had the option of not creating anything at all, if He does actualise a world where evil is done, it is implausible to say He merely allowed it.

Molinism and the Soul-Making Theodicy

Ken Perszyk writes that "it is not hard" to motivate the idea that theodicy is going to be "extra difficult" for Molinists in contrast to open theists (2013: 763). For, while Molinists, as incompatibilists about human freedom and God's determination, have the beginnings of a response to the problem of evil, we have also just seen how, on the Molinist view, God intends every evil that comes to pass, at least as part of the 'complete package'. Thus the Molinist looks committed to the idea that God must have a justifying reason for *every* evil that occurs, and these reasons must justify not merely God's *allowing* the evil that He knows will occur, but God's *positively willing* it (Rhoda 2010: 286). The question we ask now is *whether* – and if so *how* – this affects the Molinist's prospects for developing a plausible theodicy.

Our focus is on what is known as the *soul-making* theodicy, which we understand as a theodicy which incorporates the appeal to free will outlined earlier. According to John Hick, who presented the most comprehensive contemporary statement of the soul-making theodicy in his magisterial *Evil and the God of Love* (1966), the basic idea has its roots in the writings of Irenaeus. According to this theodicy humans were created not perfect, as they were on the rival Augustinian picture, but immature, and with the potential to develop morally and spiritually. God created them this way so that people could develop their own latent capacities to know and love Him, and then exercise those capacities freely.

To achieve this end God creates people at an "epistemic distance" from Himself, and in an environment containing "challenges to be met, problems to be solved, dangers to be faced, and which accordingly involves real possibilities of hardship, disaster, failure, defeat, and misery as well as of delight and happiness, success, triumph and achievement" (Hick 1990: 99). As Hick says, the value judgement in play here is that it is of great worth to become good by "meeting and mastering" temptations (2010: 255). The soul-making theodicy is like other free-will-based theodicies in that it works by positing a limitation on God's control. Indeed, the soul-making theodicy appropriates the limitation placed on God's control by human freedom, but then adds to it a further limitation based on the nature of goodness. Whereas the basic appeal to free will described earlier is premised on the idea that God must give people at least the bare choice between good and evil in order to make possible their moral agency, the soul-making theodicy adds that God must give them temptations to face in order to realise a moral goodness which "has within it the strength of temptations overcome, a stability based upon an accumulation of right choices, and a positive and responsible character that comes from the investment of costly personal effort" (Hick 2010: 255–6).

On the face of it, it looks like Molinists can appropriate this scheme without problems. Some critics, however, have contended that the Molinists' appeal to soul-making must be restricted in certain ways. As Neal Judisch explains, the issue arises from the "familiar point that not everyone who experiences trials of this sort emerges from them any better off than they were"; some become "embittered, exhausted, empty" due to suffering (2012: 73). According to Molinism, God "knows how each individual would respond to any possible trial", and this means that "God frequently allows people to suffer trials knowing they won't respond in ways conducive to soul-making" (Rhoda 2010: 296). But if God knows that someone will fail to overcome some particular evil when placed in a certain situation, and, more generally, He knows that no one will develop as a result of that particular evil, then it doesn't look as if the existence of that evil can be justified by an appeal to the value of soul-making – for by hypothesis no soul-making occurred, and God knew that no soul-making would occur when He willed the evil. The charge here isn't that Molinists can't appeal to soul-making at all; rather, it's that their appeal is limited as compared with the open theist's. For when no soul-making occurs, the open theist can "maintain [that] God permitted these persons to suffer because He thought it likely, or more probable than not, that they'd respond in salutary ways", whereas the Molinist cannot say this (Judisch 2012: 73).

Judisch offers a response to this concern on behalf of the Molinist (2012: 77–8). The charge relies on the assumption that, on the Molinist picture, *God knew the exact circumstances in which each person would, and would not, overcome any given evil suffered*. As such, God appears responsible for placing people in circumstances where they suffer evil in which no soul-making occurs. But, Judisch points out, open theists, when defending the religious adequacy of their account, are keen to stress the power and knowledge that God *does* have on their view, despite God's not knowing how each future free decision will be made. Hasker, for instance, writes, "God has complete, detailed, and utterly intimate knowledge of the entirety of the past and the present. He also, of course, knows the inward constitution, tendencies, and powers of each entity in the fullest measure" (1989: 192).

But, Judisch maintains, given this kind of knowledge, the open theist isn't in such a different position from the Molinist. If God has such "utterly intimate knowledge", then surely many of those cases in which someone suffers but no soul-making occurs will be such that God had a pretty good idea that soul-making would not occur, even if He didn't know for sure. And, if He had a pretty good idea, isn't He just as responsible – or almost as responsible for failing to prevent the situation from transpiring – as God is on the Molinist view? (2012: 77)

Judisch is surely right to highlight the stress which many open theists put on what God *does* know, and how much control He *does* have, despite not knowing the future. The more the open theist stresses the control God has, and the more the Molinist is willing to say that true CCFs place significant restrictions on what God can actualise, the closer the positions become. Still, one might think that the gap here can only be closed so far: it will always remain. For even if, on the open theist view, there are cases in which God "had a pretty good idea" that some evil would be suffered without the occurrence of any soul-making, there will also be cases in which evil is suffered without the occurrence of any soul-making but God *didn't* have a pretty good idea of what would unfold. And it seems that the open theist can appeal to a general soul-making theodicy to help to explain *those* cases whereas the Molinist cannot. Of course, *how much* of an advantage that is depends on how the details of each respective soul-making theodicy is filled in; and *whether* it is worth the costs that the Molinist believes attach to open theism is something we cannot assess here.[12]

---

[12] A similar point could be made in response to Rhoda's more general concern about Molinism quoted earlier. Rhoda says that God's intending moral evil for the sake of some greater good – what he calls an "instrumental justification of moral evil" – is "condemned in scripture". While

2.6 Theological Compatibilism and Natural Compatibilism

In Sections 2.3 and 2.4, we considered the views of two types of theological incompatibilists: open theists and Molinists. Open theism, we noted, has not been a dominant position in the Christian tradition historically, in part because its denial of complete divine foreknowledge raises questions about God's sovereign control in realising His purposes in a world containing free creatures. And some traditional theists have raised concerns about Molinism too; for to posit CCFs the truth of which are independent of what God wills would be to posit something that lies outside of God's sovereign control. This is why Reginald Garrigou-Lagrange, for example, complains that the Molinists' CCFs introduce passivity into God – because they make God's knowledge *dependent on* or *conditioned by* something "external" to Him (1949: 475–6, 529ff.; cf. Ware 2004: 64, 112).

Out of such concerns for God's sovereign control and independence from the created world, many theists have been led to insist on a deterministic picture of divine providence. Since most theological determinists want to avoid free will scepticism, they must be theological compatibilists. But in Section 2.2 we argued against the view of those who contend that free will is compatible with theological determinism, but incompatible with natural determinism. Thus theological determinists must be thoroughgoing compatibilists – that is, they must assume that free will is compatible with natural as well as theological determinism. This section considers those who embrace such a position. We call this position NT-compatibilism (for natural and theological compatibilism).

It's crucial to see that compatibilism – natural or theological – says nothing about in what free will consists. Up until now we have assumed that free will consists in having a choice between alternatives. Many compatibilists – of all stripes – agree with this understanding of free will.[13] In non-theological circles

---

much could be said about how this scriptural condemnation of a certain kind of human motivation might (or might not) set constraints on *God's* intentions, our point is that an open theist view of providence *might* face a similar problem, depending on how the details of the view are fleshed out. If God knows that there is a 95 per cent chance that a created person will sin if put in a particular situation, and God puts that person in that situation for the sake of some greater good, then it would seem fair to say that God *intends* the person's sin. Then again, if God doesn't know any such precise probabilities about the future free choices of created persons, or if the probabilities are much lower (say, 50 per cent), then the language of divine *intention* of moral evil might not be appropriate on the open theist's view.

[13] This position – natural compatibilism combined with choice-based free will – is often called 'classical compatibilism' (Berofsky (2003); Todd and Fischer (2015: 8)); however, some contemporary philosophers use 'classical compatibilism' to refer to early formulations of compatibilism by such thinkers as Hobbes and Hume (Kane 1996: 61; McKenna & Coates 2015: 13–20). We therefore avoid the term.

natural compatibilists who take free will to involve a choice between alternatives include George F. Moore (1912), Alfred J. Ayer (1977: 318), Patrick H. Nowell-Smith (1960), Joseph K. Campbell (1997) and Kadri Vihvelin (2013). The popularity of this position has declined in recent decades due to the influence of Peter Strawson (2003) and Frankfurt (1969).

This decline led to a proliferation of accounts of free will that do not involve a choice between alternatives. Such accounts include Frankfurt's own hierarchical account (1971), briefly discussed in the previous section (see Section 1.2.1). Christian philosopher Lynne Rudder Baker proposed an account similar to Frankfurt's according to which a person S does X freely if "(i) S wills X, (ii) S wants to will X, (iii) S wills X because she wants to will X, and (iv) S would still have willed X even if she (herself) had known the provenance of her wanting to will X" (2003: 467). Baker is clear that on her account "a person S's having free will with respect to an action (or choice) A is compatible with A's being caused ultimately by factors outside of S's control" (2003: 460). Moreover, it makes no difference whether the agent's action is deterministically caused "by God or by natural events" (2003: 461). Many theologians and theistic philosophers defend such views, often finding precedence for them in the Christian tradition. For example, Jesse Couenhoven (2013) and Ian McFarland (2010), as well as Baker, engage with Augustine's writings to defend views according to which free will does not require choice.

Perhaps surprisingly, however, the details of these different accounts of free will need not concern us here. That's because most debates about what, exactly, free will consists in and whether it is compatible with determinism occur outside of philosophy of religion, since the considerations raised in favour and against the different views are unrelated to theistic commitments. Thus, in the first part of this section, we assume that free will – whatever it consists in – is compatible with natural and theological determinism, and consider whether the NT-compatibilist can make any appeal to free will when developing a theodicy. Then, in the second part, we go on to consider whether NT-compatibilism compromises God's standing to blame.

NT-Compatibilism, Free Will and the Problem of Evil

The biggest challenge facing theological determinists in general, and NT-compatibilists in particular, is the problem of evil. For if God *causes, determines, decrees, brings about* or *settles* everything that comes to pass (as we've seen, determinists vary according to which verbs they're happy to endorse here), then God would seem to be as intimately involved in moral evil as He could be, short of performing the evil actions Himself.

Moreover, most contemporary theological determinists who endorse NT-compatibilism acknowledge that an appeal to creaturely free will is of no help to them in solving the problem (Alexander & Johnson 2016: 12). That's because, according to NT-compatibilism, God can determine precisely what any person freely chooses at any time, and so has the power to make every creature always freely choose the good. This is why John S. Feinberg, an NT-compatibilist, writes, "I don't answer the problem of evil by the free will defence ... because I hold a compatibilist account of free will" (2004: 165).

There are, however, a few dissenters to this majority view. One is T. Ryan Byerly, who has argued that determinists *can* appropriate large parts of Plantinga's free will defence, Hick's soul-making theodicy and Swinburne's free will-based "moral knowledge" theodicy, all of which are explicitly incompatibilist (Byerly 2017). We focus here on Byerly's treatment of Hick.

The central idea of the soul-making theodicy, which we summarised in Section 2.5, is that a particular kind of moral goodness is only possible for a person who has faced and freely overcome evil. Although Hick thinks free will is incompatible with both natural and theological determinism, Byerly's aim is to show that enough of Hick's picture can be adopted by the theological determinist in order to challenge the "widespread view" that an adequate response to the problem of evil requires theological incompatibilism (2017: 289, 292).

Byerly thinks that it's "not difficult" to see how the theological compatibilist could appropriate Hick's theodicy. For the theological compatibilist "may affirm that inculcating a virtuous character by means of performing free acts productive of virtue is a great freedom good", and that "this is a freedom good that can only be achieved by God through permitting evils to occur", because it is only in the face of such evils that these character-forming actions can take place (2017: 292). Indeed, Byerly suggests that:

> The only difference between [the theological compatibilist] and Hick is that [the former] thinks that those free actions created agents perform in response to these evils are acts that are causally determined to occur. Hick may say these acts are for this reason not free ... [b]ut, since the theological determinist affirms that free action is compatible with causal determinism, she needs not concede this point. (2017: 292)

When Byerly says that "the only difference" is that the compatibilist thinks the free actions creatures perform are causally determined, he seems to mean that *this difference has no further consequences*. However, this difference has significant consequences for *which* evils the appeal to soul-making can justify.

Here's why. If God can control how each creature freely decides, as He can according to the theological determinist, then the soul-making theodicy can only be used to explain the existence of those evils necessary for soul-making. For example, suppose that to develop courage, there needs to be evils of kind E1 or worse. Then God would be justified in creating or allowing evils of kind E1 to facilitate the developing of courage (assuming the development of courage outweighs evils of kind E1, of course). But suppose that evils of kind E2 also exist which are worse than evils of kind E1. It would seem that God would not be justified in creating or allowing evils of kind E2 to facilitate the learning of courage in His creatures, given that, by hypothesis, He could do so with evils of kind E1 instead. So, in any situation where the evil seems to be greater than that required to facilitate whatever soul-making occurs, the theological compatibilist will be unable to use soul-making to justify the existence of that evil.

The incompatibilist soul-making theodicy does not have this limitation, however. That's because part of the claim of the theodicy is that soul-making occurs only when creatures *freely make* character-forming decisions. And, the incompatibilist will maintain, since free will is incompatible with God's determining activity, God cannot prevent humans from making evil decisions without removing their free will. But that means, in turn, that the theological incompatibilist can say the following: free will is needed for moral decisions to be made. And for soul-making purposes, certain evils, such as those of kind E1, are needed, because such evils are necessary for the development of certain virtues. Unfortunately, the incompatibilist will continue, God's bestowing free will on people, which makes possible the development of those virtues, also inevitably brings with it the possibility of their committing other evils, such as those of kind E2. And these may be justified by the collective moral growth that occurs, even though evils of kind E2 aren't necessary for such growth. We should make clear that our claim is not that the incompatibilist who deploys the soul-making theodicy *must* appeal to soul-making to explain every moral evil in this manner. Our claim is simply that the incompatibilist soul-making theodicist can justify *some* evils committed by free creatures that are not necessary for the actual soul-making that occurs, and that therefore the incompatibilist has an advantage over the compatibilist.

A compatibilist version of the soul-making theodicy must also rely on a value claim that an incompatibilist need not assume. For the compatibilist must admit that God *can* create people who are free and yet guarantee that they are (and remain) morally perfect, in the sense that they always make the right choice. Thus the compatibilist will have to say that the *particular kind* of moral character that can be developed through encountering and overcoming evils is of such value that it outweighs the disvalue of all of those evils. To put the point differently, the compatibilist must say that a world in which people can develop that particular kind of moral character – and in which there is thus much evil – is better than a world in which people are created morally perfect and so in which no moral evil exists. Incompatibilists do not have to make such a value claim, for they think that it is *not* possible for God to create free people and guarantee that they be morally perfect. Thus incompatibilists need only claim that any/all kinds of moral agency or goodness outweigh the existence of moral evil – not some particular kind that is developed through meeting and mastering temptations. Whether or not one finds plausible the value claim that compatibilist soul-making theodicists must assume, it is an added burden for the view.

We have only considered here how one popular free-will-based theodicy might be revised to work as an NT-compatibilist theodicy of moral evil. Compatibilists could try in other ways to appropriate an appeal to free will. But the foregoing considerations suggest that compatibilist free-will-based theodicies are likely to require additional assumptions that may be questioned, and are unlikely to be able to account for as much evil as incompatibilist free-will-based theodicies are. This accords with the general consensus mentioned in the previous subsection, namely, that NT-compatibilists are better off making some other sort of response to the problem of moral evil.

It is worth noting here that, while theological incompatibilists and *some* NT-compatibilists will see our conclusion as a challenge that the NT-compatibilist must overcome, other NT-compatibilists will not see that conclusion as particularly worrying. For many are convinced on independent grounds that free will simply cannot do the 'heavy lifting' that it's expected to do in most free-will-based theodicies. We noted in Section 2.3 that Ekstrom has challenged the value claim that free will and the moral responsibility it makes possible are 'worth' all the evil that free creatures commit. Adams has suggested another reason why free will is not up to the task that free-will-based theodicies demand of it, having to do with the *fragility* of human life and the *vulnerability* of human agency (including free agency) (2006: 38). On the one hand, she points out, human life is fragile in the sense that that we are extremely susceptible to significant harm, and on the other, human agency is vulnerable in the sense that it is very easy to become a perpetrator of "horrors", or evils that can destroy a person's "meaning-making capacities" (2006: 33). Adams illustrates these points with an example based on a famous passage in Dostoyevsky's *The Brothers Karamazov*: teenage soldiers who, lacking "the empathetic capacity to experience anything like enough to match the mother's anguish", threw babies into the air and caught them on bayonets (2006: 35). Since agents such as these cannot fully understand "how bad are the evils" they commit, it follows that they "cannot be fully morally responsible for the horrors [they] perpetuate" (2006: 35). Thus, free-will-based theodicies that attempt to "shift responsibility ... for evil from God and onto personal creatures ... are stalemated by horrendous evil" (2006: 36).

Finally, we note that the theological determinist might make other responses to the problem of evil; two which have received recent, well-developed exposition are sceptical theism (see Part 3 of McBrayer and Howard-Snyder 2013) and the divine glory defence (see e.g. Johnson 2016).

God's Standing to Blame

We turn now to a problem for compatibilism recently formulated by Patrick Todd (2012). Although it is presented as a challenge primarily for natural compatibilists, it also applies to NT-compatibilists and, indeed, it requires the possibility that theological determinism is true. The problem goes like this: traditional theism affirms not only that God is good, and not at fault for any evil in the world He created, but also that God is *opposed to wrongdoing* in the sense that *He condemns it*. Now, assuming that the NT-compatibilist can explain how a God who determines people to commit blameworthy acts could Himself be blameless, still, a further question remains: can such a God *Himself* justifiably blame people? Call this 'the problem of divine standing to blame'.

The question of whether a deterministic Creator could justifiably blame His creatures is distinct from the question of whether those creatures could be blameworthy. For it may be that someone meets the conditions necessary for being responsible for her own actions, and so is liable to blame, and yet some third party is not *in a position* to blame her. Yet Todd argues that (1) a deterministic God could not justifiably blame His creatures for wrongdoing, even if they met "all the compatibilist conditions for being morally responsible", and (2) the best explanation for (1) is that compatibilism is false: creatures who were determined to act would not be responsible for what they do, and so would not be liable to blame (2012: 5).[14] If Todd's conclusion is correct, this would obviously be a problem for the theological determinist-compatibilist – and for compatibilists more generally, who acknowledge at least the logical possibility of a Creator who determines human actions.

Todd spends most of his energies defending premise (2) of his argument. He considers two other sorts of reasons why someone might lack standing to blame

---

[14] Todd (2018) inverts this argument, contending that God *does* have standing to blame on a theological deterministic picture of providence *if compatibilism is true*.

another – besides that the other is not, in fact, responsible for wrongdoing – and finds them both inapplicable in the case of theological determinism. The first possible reason is that the blamer is blaming in bad faith, because her actions reveal that she doesn't really care about the values that undergird her criticism of the blamed party. One might charge, for instance, that God cannot blame a person for committing murder, because the fact that God determined the person to commit murder shows that God doesn't really care about human life or respect for persons (2012: 7). But, Todd notes, an adequate theodicy would show that God *does* care about the values undergirding His criticism. That God determines someone to commit murder shows not that God approves of such an action in itself, or considers it good in itself, but only that God judges that it contributes to some greater good, or is necessary to prevent some greater evil (2012: 7–8).

The second reason why someone might lack standing to blame another for wrongdoing is that the blamer is somehow involved in the wrong done. But, Todd argues, such involvement removes one's standing to blame only if the one involved is *at fault*, in the sense of having done wrong by being involved (2012: 9). Todd considers a (fictitious) case of a Nazi commander who orders an alarm to be sounded in response to rumours of an escape attempt at a death camp, and then later blames the underling who obeyed his order. If the commander was secretly working against the Nazi regime, and only gave the order to sound the alarm because he thought doing so was the possible action that would have the least bad consequences for the prisoners, then he would not be at fault for giving the order – and, Todd suggests, he would be justified in blaming the underling who obeyed it (2012: 10–11). Just so, on the assumption that there is an adequate theodicy that would absolve a deterministic God of wrongdoing for causing people to do wrong, it follows that God would not lack standing to blame for this reason either.

Todd concludes that since blaming in bad faith, and blaming while at fault, are the two alternative conditions that might undermine one's status to blame, and since neither of these applies to God on the theological determinist picture, what in fact undermines God's status to blame must be that those blamed are not responsible for what they do. And the reason they are not responsible, of course, is that God's determination of their action is *incompatible* with responsibility. Thus, compatibilism is false.

John Ross Churchill has offered one response to Todd's argument on behalf of the theological compatibilist. Churchill acknowledges the apparent difficulty with divine blame on a theological determinist account. But he provides an alternative explanation for why such divine blame at least *seems* problematic. He then goes on to argue that if divine blame is correctly understood, it is not unjustified on theological determinism. In offering his alternative explanation Churchill quotes Todd's imagined case of divine blame:

> Suppose you "wake up" to find yourself in an afterlife, during which time it is somehow made clear that everything you ever did was part of a divinely preordained plan. And then God says to you: "You know, what you did on this occasion was really a horrible thing to have done. What's your excuse? How could you?" Isn't there something deeply unsettling about this scenario? Wouldn't you suppose that something had gone completely wrong? (Todd, as cited in Churchill 2017: 431)

Churchill agrees with Todd that what is unsettling about the scenario is not that God is blaming in bad faith or while at fault. But he proposes that the problem is that God seems insincere. For when God says "What's your excuse? How could you?" he seems to be demanding an explanation for bad behaviour while at the same time assuming there is no justification, but rather expecting that the blamed party will end up admitting wrongdoing. "Indeed", Churchill writes, "the questions are more like expressions of *shock* or *incredulity* at my behaviour than requests for information. And ... surely the God who has determined me to sin ... cannot sincerely confront me with anything like shocked or incredulous demands that I explain that very sin" (2017: 433–4).

Churchill notes that if the problem with divine blame concerns God's apparent insincerity in blaming, then "it is a problem that specifically concerns *God's* standing to blame those who have been divinely determined, rather than threatening to undermine the legitimacy of all blame everywhere by challenging the moral responsibility of all agents" (2017: 435). If he is right, then NT-compatibilists are out of the woods, though theological determinists who affirm divine blame still have a challenge to face. But Churchill goes on to address this challenge by arguing that divine blame need not involve such insincerity. For while expressions of shock or incredulity are common to ordinary blaming practices, they are not universal to blame, and divine blame need not involve such expressions. Churchill discusses various accounts of blame including cognitive approaches, which emphasise the role of negative evaluations of the blamed person's character or will, and affective approaches, which prioritise the role of emotions such as anger or resentment. He writes, "at least some of our blaming behavior manifests either or both of the requisite cognitive or affective features, *but does not include explicit explanatory demands of those blamed*" (2017: 435).

While Churchill is right that not *all* blame involves such demands, on the traditional theistic view God's blaming, at least sometimes, does. And the alternative models of blame that Churchill discusses seem either insufficient, or inappropriate, at least when it comes to divine blame. Cognitive approaches clearly capture *something* about blame, whether human or divine. But blame typically involves more than a simple *judgement*. When we read a student paper that has been plagiarised, we form the judgement that the student has done wrong, and that this reflects something negative about the student's character (that he is dishonest, or lazy, or whatever); but we do not, in judging so, blame the student. Our blame only comes later, when we confront the student to tell him why he is receiving a failing grade for the assignment: because he is at fault for what he has done, since he knew better and had the capacity to write the essay himself. In other words, our act of blaming is at least in part aimed at getting the student to admit wrongdoing. While such cases need not involve expressions of shock or incredulity, the insistence that the blamed party *should have known and done better* would seem just as insincere, coming from the One who determined the bad behaviour.

Affective approaches to divine blame also seem inappropriate. As Churchill mentions in a footnote, "Classical theologians count ascriptions of emotion . . . to God as mere anthropopathisms" (2017: n. 32). Nevertheless, he goes on to insist that an affective approach to divine blame is unproblematic, since talk of divine emotions can be reinterpreted as talk of divine *actions* (2017: n. 32). If that's right, however, then it's unclear how this reinterpretation counts as an affective approach at all. Moreover, the divine actions that Churchill suggests substituting for emotions in the reinterpretation – God's negative judgement of the bad behaviour or denouncement of the wrongdoer – return us to problems discussed earlier: divine blame would seem to involve, at least in many cases, more than a negative judgement, and denouncement of an offender suggests an explanatory demand or expression of shock.

It seems, then, that God's blaming those He determines really would be insincere. What is more, when Churchill asserts that it is the apparent insincerity of such divine blame that makes it seem inappropriate, he takes this to be an alternative explanation to Todd's proposal of incompatibilism, since, as mentioned earlier, such insincerity has the potential to undermine only *God's* standing to blame us, and not our standing to blame each other. However, the apparent insincerity of God's blaming and the truth of incompatibilism are not necessarily distinct explanations for the inappropriateness of divine blame on theological determinism. For if everything in the world is determined by God, then God surely knows this, and knows exactly what we will do. This is why – the incompatibilist can argue – it is insincere of God to tell us that we should have done better – because He knows that, in the relevant sense, we could not! But *we* do not know either that everything we do is in fact determined, or what we will in fact do. The incompatibilist can maintain that if we had the kind of knowledge that a deterministic God would have, it would seem equally insincere for us to blame each other.

Churchill may not share this intuition, of course. And that brings us to a larger point about the dialectic. Todd's argument basically *assumes* that a deterministic God could not justifiably blame His creatures for wrongdoing (premise (1) of his argument). After offering the thought experiment discussed earlier, Todd writes, "In the end, it simply seems to me that if God determines us to perform an action, he cannot blame us for having performed it. I do not know how to argue for this claim. I simply say that it is eminently plausible" (2012: 16). If this is eminently plausible, though, then why do so many theological determinists deny it? Todd suggests that the fact that theological determinists generally affirm the appropriateness of divine blame is simply "testimony to the sometimes incredible power religious commitments can have in leading people to accept what would otherwise seem to be overwhelmingly implausible" (2012: 17). There is, perhaps, an element of truth here. But a more charitable interpretation might be that theological compatibilists are committed to a worldview which contributes to the production of intuitions in line with that worldview. That is, it's not that their religious commitments are simply *overriding* their intuitions, but rather, that those commitments are helping to *form* their intuitions (or, perhaps, it's some of both). The point is this. Todd's argument might persuade – or at least give pause to – some merely natural compatibilists. But it is unlikely to have much traction against NT-compatibilists, as such compatibilists are likely already 'on board' with the idea that God blames us for the evil that He determines us to do.

Bibliography

Adams, M. M. (1967). Is the Existence of God a 'Hard' Fact? *The Philosophical Review*, *76*(4), 492–503.

Adams, M. M. (2006). *Christ and Horrors: The Coherence of Christology*. Cambridge: Cambridge University Press.

Alexander, D. E., & Johnson, D. M. (2016). Introduction. In D. E. Alexander & D. M. Johnson (eds.), *Calvinism and the Problem of Evil* (pp. 1–18). Eugene, OR: Pickwick Publications.

Ayer, A. J. (1977). Freedom and Necessity. In R. Abelson, M.-L. Friquegnon & M. Lockwood (eds.), *The Philosophical Imagination*. (pp. 311–19). New York: St. Martin's Press.

Baker, L. R. (2003). Why Christians Should Not Be Libertarians: An Augustinian Challenge. *Faith and Philosophy*, *20*(4), 460–78.

Basinger, D. (1994). Practical Implications. In C. H. Pinnock (ed.), *The Openness of God: A Biblical Challenge to the Traditional Understanding of God* (pp. 155–76). Downers Grove, IL: InterVarsity Press.

Berofsky, B. (2003). Classical Compatibilism: Not Dead Yet. In M. S. McKenna & D. Widerker (eds.), *Moral Responsibility and Alternative Possibilities* (pp. 107–27). Aldershot: Ashgate.

Boethius. (1999). *The Consolation of Philosophy*. London: Penguin.

Boyd, G. A. (2001a). *God of the Possible: A Biblical Introduction to the Open View of God*. Grand Rapids, MI: Baker Books.

Boyd, G. A. (2001b). *Satan and the Problem of Evil: Constructing a Trinitarian Warfare Theodicy*. Downers Grove, IL: InterVarsity Press.

Boyd, G. A. (2001c). The Open-Theism View. In P. R. Eddy & J. K. Beilby (eds.), *Divine Foreknowledge: Four Views* (pp. 13–47). Carlisle: Paternoster Press.

Boyd, G. A. (2011). God Limits His Control. In D. W. Jowers (ed.), *Four Views on Divine Providence* (pp. 183–208). Grand Rapids, MI: Zondervan.

Byerly, T. R. (2017). Free Will Theodicies for Theological Determinists. *Sophia*, *56*(2), 289–310.

Campbell, J. K. (1997). A Compatibilist Theory of Alternative Possibilities. *Philosophical Studies*, *88*(3), 319–30.

Churchill, J. R. (2017). Determinism and Divine Blame. *Faith and Philosophy*, *34*(4), 425–48.

Coburn, R. C. (1963). Professor Malcolm on God. *Australasian Journal of Philosophy*, *41*(2), 143–62.

Cohen, Y. (2014). Molinists (Still) Cannot Endorse the Consequence Argument. *International Journal for Philosophy of Religion*. OnlineFirst. *77*(3), 231–46.

Couenhoven, J. (2013). *Stricken by Sin, Cured by Christ*. New York: Oxford University Press USA.

Crabtree, J. A. (2004). *The Most Real Being: A Biblical and Philosophical Defense of Divine Determinism*. Eugene, OR: Gutenberg College Press.

Craig, W. L. (1987). *The Only Wise God*. Eugene, OR: Wipf and Stock Publishers.

Craig, W. L. (1989). 'No Other Name': A Middle Knowledge Perspective on the Exclusivity of Salvation through Christ. *Faith and Philosophy*, *6*(2), 172–88.

Craig, W. L. (1999). "Men Moved by the Holy Spirit Spoke from God": A Middle Knowledge Perspective on Biblical Inspiration. *Philosophia Christi*, *1*(1), 45–82.

Craig, W. L. (2001). The Middle-Knowledge View. In P. R. Eddy & J. K. Beilby (eds.), *Divine Foreknowledge: Four Views* (pp. 119–43). Carlisle: Paternoster Press.

Craig, W. L. (2017). A Molinist View. In C. V. Meister & J. K. Dew Jr (eds.), *God and the Problem of Evil: Five Views*. Downers Grove, IL: IVP Academic.

Ekstrom, L. W. (2016). The Cost of Freedom. In K. Timpe & D. Speak (eds.), *Free Will and Theism* (pp. 62–78). Oxford: Oxford University Press.

Feinberg, J. S. (2004). *The Many Faces of Evil: Theological Systems and the Problems of Evil* (Rev. and expanded edn). Wheaton, IL: Crossway Books.

Fischer, J. M. (1986). Power Necessity. *Philosophical Topics*, *14*(2), 77–91.

Fischer, J. M. (1989). Introduction. In J. M. Fischer (ed.), *God, Foreknowledge, and Freedom* (pp. 1–56). Stanford, CA: Stanford University Press.

Fischer, J. M. (1992). Recent Work on God and Freedom. *American Philosophical Quarterly*, *29*(2), 91–109.

Fischer, J. M. (2016a). Introduction. In J. M. Fischer (ed.), *Our Fate: Essays on God and Free Will* (pp. 1–52). Oxford: Oxford University Press.

Fischer, J. M. (2016b). Ockhamism: The Facts. In J. M. Fischer (ed.), *Our Fate: Essays on God and Free Will* (pp. 130–49). Oxford: Oxford University Press.

Fischer, J. M. (ed.). (1989a). *God, Foreknowledge, and Freedom*. Stanford, CA: Stanford University Press.

Fischer, J. M., & Todd, P. (2011) The Truth about Freedom. A Reply to Merricks. *The Philosophical Review*, *120*(1), 97–115.

Fischer, J. M., & Tognazzini, N. A. (2014). Omniscience, Freedom, and Dependence. *Philosophy and Phenomenological Research*, *88*(2), 346–67.

Flint, T. P. (1998). *Divine Providence: The Molinist Account*. Ithaca, NY: Cornell University Press.

Flint, T. P. (1999). A New Anti-Anti-Molinist Argument. *Religious Studies*, *35*(3), 299–305.

Flint, T. P. (2011). Divine Providence. In T. P. Flint & M. C. Rea (eds.), *The Oxford Handbook of Philosophical Theology* (pp. 262–85). New York: Oxford University Press.

Frankfurt, H. G. (1969). Alternate Possibilities and Moral Responsibility. *Journal of Philosophy*, *66*(3), 829–39.

Frankfurt, H. G. (1971). Freedom of the Will and the Concept of a Person. *The Journal of Philosophy*, *68*(1), 5–20.

Frankfurt, H. G. (1988). *The Importance of What We Care About: Philosophical Essays*. Cambridge: Cambridge University Press.

Freddoso, A. J. (1983). Accidental Necessity and Logical Determinism. *Journal of Philosophy*, *80*(5), 257–78.

Freddoso, A. J. (1988). Introduction. In A. J. Freddoso (ed.), *On Divine Foreknowledge: Part IV of the Concordia* (pp. 1–81). Ithaca, NY: Cornell University Press.

Garrigou-Lagrange, R. (1949). *God: His Existence and Nature: Volume 2* (5th edn). St. Louis, MO: B. Herder Book Company.

Ginet, C. (1990). *On Action*. Cambridge: Cambridge University Press.

Grant, W. M. (2010). Can a Libertarian Hold That Our Free Acts Are Caused by God? *Faith and Philosophy*, *27*(1), 22–44.

Grant, W. M. (2016). Divine Universal Causality and Libertarian Freedom. In K. Timpe & D. Speak (eds.), *Free Will and Theism* (pp. 214–33). Oxford: Oxford University Press.

Grössl, J., & Vicens, L. (2014). Closing the Door on Limited-Risk Open Theism. *Faith and Philosophy*, *31*(4), 475–85.

Hasker, W. (1988). Hard Facts and Theological Fatalism. *Noûs*, *22*(3), 419–36.

Hasker, W. (1989). *God, Time, and Knowledge*. Ithaca, NY: Cornell University Press.

Hasker, W. (1992). Providence and Evil: Three Theories. *Religious Studies*, *28*(1), 91–105.

Hasker, W. (1994). A Philosophical Perspective. In C. H. Pinnock (ed.), *The Openness of God: A Biblical Challenge to the Traditional Understanding of God* (pp. 126–54). Downers Grove, IL: InterVarsity Press.

Hasker, W. (1999). A New Anti-Molinist Argument. *Religious Studies*, *35*(3), 291–7.

Hasker, W. (2001). The Foreknowledge Conundrum. *International Journal for Philosophy of Religion*, *50*(1/3), 97–114.

Hasker, W. (2004). *Providence, Evil and the Openness of God*. Oxford: Routledge.

Hasker, W. (2011). Theological Incompatibilism and the Necessity of the Present. *Faith and Philosophy, 28*(2), 224–9.

Helm, P. (2004). God Does Not Take Risks. In M. L. Peterson & R. J. VanArragon (eds.), *Contemporary Debates in Philosophy of Religion* (pp. 228–37). Malden, MA: Blackwell.

Hick, J. (1966). *Evil and the God of Love*. Basingstoke: Palgrave Macmillan.

Hick, J. (1990). An Irenaean Theodicy. In P. Badham (ed.), *A John Hick Reader* (pp. 88–105). Basingstoke: Macmillan.

Hick, J. (2010). *Evil and the God of Love* (Reissued with a new preface). Basingstoke: Palgrave Macmillan.

Himma, K. E. (2009). The Free Will Defence: Evil and the Moral Value of Free Will. *Religious Studies, 45*(4), 395–415.

Hobbes, T., Bramhall, J. & Chappell, V. C. (1999). *Thomas Hobbes and John Bramhall: On Liberty and Necessity*. Cambridge: Cambridge University Press.

Hoffman, J., & Rosenkrantz, G. S. (1984). Hard and Soft Facts. *The Philosophical Review, 93*(3), 419–34.

Hoffman, J. & Rosenkrantz, G. S. (2002). *The Divine Attributes*. Oxford: John Wiley & Sons.

Howard-Snyder, D. (1996). Introduction: The Evidential Argument from Evil. In D. Howard-Snyder (ed.), *The Evidential Argument from Evil* (pp. 19–55). Bloomington: Indiana University Press.

Johnson, D. M. (2016). Calvinism and the Problem of Evil. In D. E. Alexander & D. M. Johnson (eds.), *Calvinism and the Problem of Evil*. Eugene, OR: Pickwick Publications.

Johnson, D. K. (2009). God, Fatalism, and Temporal Ontology. *Religious Studies, 45*(4), 435–54.

Judisch, N. (2012). Meticulous Providence and Gratuitous Evil. In J. L. Kvanvig (ed.), *Oxford Studies in Philosophy of Religion: Volume 4* (pp. 65–83). Oxford: Oxford University Press.

Kane, R. H. (1996). *The Significance of Free Will* (New edn). New York: Oxford University Press USA.

Kvanvig, J. L. (1986). *The Possibility of an All-Knowing God*. London: Macmillan.

Mackie, J. L. (1955). Evil and Omnipotence. *Mind, 64*(254), 200–12.

Mavrodes, G. I. (1984). Is the Past Unpreventable? *Faith and Philosophy, 1*(2), 131–46.

Mavrodes, G. I. (2010). Omniscience. In P. Draper, P. L. Quinn & C. Taliaferro (eds.), *A Companion to Philosophy of Religion* (2nd edn, pp. 251–7). Malden, MA: Wiley-Blackwell.

McBrayer, J. P., & Howard-Snyder, D. (eds.). (2013). *The Blackwell Companion to the Problem of Evil*. Malden, MA: Wiley Blackwell.

McCabe, L. D. (1882). *Divine Nescience of Future Contingents a Necessity*. New York: Phillips and Hunt.

McCall, S. (2011). The Supervenience of Truth. Freewill and Omniscience, *Analysis*, *71*(3), 501–6.

McCann, H. J. (1995). Divine Sovereignty and the Freedom of the Will. *Faith and Philosophy*, *12*(4), 582–98.

McCann, H. J. (2001). Sovereignty and Freedom: A Reply to Rowe. *Faith and Philosophy*, *18*(1), 110–16.

McCann, H. J., & Johnson, D. M. (2017). Divine Providence. In E. N. Zalta (ed.), *Stanford Encyclopedia of Philosophy*.

McFarland, I. A. (2010). *In Adam's Fall: A Meditation on the Christian Doctrine of Original Sin*. Oxford: Wiley-Blackwell.

McKay, T., & Johnson, D. (1996). A Reconsideration of an Argument against Compatibilism. *Philosophical Topics*, *24*(2), 113–22.

McKenna, M. S., & Coates, D. J. (2015). Compatibilism. In E. N. Zalta (ed.), *Stanford Encyclopedia of Philosophy*. Winter 2015 edn. https://plato .stanford.edu/archives/win2015/entries/compatibilism/>

Merricks, T. (2009). Truth and Freedom. *The Philosophical Review*, *118*(1), 29–57.

Moore, G. E. (1912). *Ethics*. London: Humphrey Milford.

Nouwen, H. J. M. (1996). *Bread for the Journey*. London: Darton, Longman and Todd.

Nowell-Smith, P. H. (1960). Ifs and Cans. *Theoria*, *26*, 85–101.

O'Connor, T. (1993). On the Transfer of Necessity. *Noûs*, *27*(2), 204–18.

Pereboom, D. (2009). Free Will, Evil, and Divine Providence. In A. Dole & A. Chignell (eds.), *God and the Ethics of Belief* (pp. 77–98). Cambridge: Cambridge University Press.

Pereboom, D. (2016). Libertarianism and Theological Determinism. In K. Timpe & D. Speak (eds.), *Free Will and Theism* (pp. 112–31). Oxford: Oxford University Press.

Perszyk, K. (2013). Recent Work on Molinism. *Philosophy Compass*, *8*(8), 755–70.

Pike, N. (1965). Divine Omniscience and Voluntary Action. *The Philosophical Review*, *74*(1), 27–46.

Pike, N. (1970). *God and Timelessness*. London: Routledge & Kegan Paul.

Pink, A. W. (1949). *The Sovereignty of God* (4th edn). Grand Rapids, MI: Christian Classics Ethereal Library.

Pinnock, C. H. (ed.). (1994). *The Openness of God*. Downers Grove, IL: InterVarsity Press.

Pinnock, C. H., Rice, R., Sanders, J., Hasker, W., & Basinger, D. (1994). Preface. In C. H. Pinnock (cd.), *The Openness of God* (pp. 1–10). Downers Grove, IL: InterVarsity Press.

Plantinga, A. (1978). *The Nature of Necessity* (New edn). Oxford: Clarendon Press.

Plantinga, A. (1986). On Ockham's Way Out. *Faith and Philosophy, 3*(3), 235–69.

Rhoda, A. R. (2010). Gratuitous Evil and Divine Providence. *Religious Studies, 46*(3), 281–302.

Rice, R. (1980). *The Openness of God: The Relationship of Divine Foreknowledge and Human Free Will.* Nashville, TN: Review and Herald Publishing Association.

Rice, R. (1985). *God's Foreknowledge & Man's Free Will* (1st edn). Minneapolis, MN: Bethany House.

Rice, R. (1994). Biblical Support for a New Perspective. In C. H. Pinnock (ed.), *The Openness of God* (pp. 11–58). Downers Grove, IL: InterVarsity Press.

Rogers, K. A. (2007a). Anselmian Eternalism. *Faith and Philosophy, 24*(1), 3–27.

Rogers, K. A. (2007b). The Necessity of the Present and Anselm's Eternalist Response to the Problem of Theological Fatalism. *Religious Studies, 43*(1), 25–47.

Rowe, W. L. (1979). The Problem of Evil and Some Varieties of Atheism. *American Philosophical Quarterly, 16*(4), 335–41.

Rowe, W. L. (1996). The Evidential Argument from Evil: A Second Look. In D. Howard-Snyder (ed.), *The Evidential Argument from Evil* (pp. 262–85). Bloomington: Indiana University Press.

Rowling, J. K. (2015). *Harry Potter and the Chamber of Secrets.* London: Bloomsbury.

Sanders, J. (2007). *The God Who Risks* (2nd edn). Downers Grove, IL: IVP Academic.

Shanley, B. J. (1998). Divine Causation and Human Freedom in Aquinas. *American Catholic Philosophical Quarterly, 72*(1), 99–122.

Speak, D. J. (2011). The Consequence Argument Revisited. In R. H. Kane (ed.), *The Oxford Handbook of Free Will* (2nd edn, pp. 115–30). Oxford: Oxford University Press.

Strawson, P. F. (2003). Freedom and Resentment. In G. Watson (ed.), *Free Will* (2nd edn). Oxford: Oxford University Press (Original work published 1962).

Stump, E. (1996). Persons: Identification and Freedom. *Philosophical Topics, 24*(2) Free Will (Fall), 183–214.

Swinburne, R. (1977). *The Coherence of Theism* (1st edn). New York: Oxford University Press, USA.

Swinburne, R. (2016). *The Coherence of Theism* (2nd edn). Oxford: Oxford University Press.

Tanner, K. E. (1994). Human Freedom, Human Sin, and God the Creator. In T. F. Tracy (ed.), *The God Who Acts* (pp. 111–35). University Park: Pennsylvania State University Press.

Todd, P. (2012). Manipulation and Moral Standing. *Philosophers' Imprint*, *12*(7), 1–18.

Todd, P. (2013). Soft Facts and Ontological Dependence. *Philosophical Studies*, *164*(3), 829–44.

Todd, P. (2018). Does God Have the Moral Standing to Blame? *Faith and Philosophy*, *35*(1), 33–55.

Todd, P., & Fischer, J. M. (2015). Introduction. In J. M. Fischer & P. Todd (eds.), *Freedom, Fatalism, and Foreknowledge* (1st edn, pp. 1–38). Oxford: Oxford University Press.

Van Inwagen, P. (1983). *An Essay on Free Will*. Oxford: Clarendon Press.

Van Inwagen, P. (1989). When Is the Will Free? *Philosophical Perspectives*, *3*, 399–422.

Van Inwagen, P. (2008). What Does an Omniscient Being Know about the Future? In J. L. Kvanvig (ed.), *Oxford Studies in Philosophy of Religion: Volume 1* (pp. 216–30). Oxford: Oxford University Press.

Vierkant, T., Kiverstein, J. & Clark, A. (2013). Decomposing the Will: Meeting the Zombie Challenge. In A. Clark, J. Kiverstein & T. Vierkant (eds.), *Decomposing the Will* (pp. 1–30). New York: Oxford University Press, USA.

Vihvelin, K. (2013). *Causes, Laws, and Free Will: Why Determinism Doesn't Matter*. New York: Oxford University Press.

Ware, B. A. (2001). *God's Lesser Glory*. Leicester: Inter-Varsity Press.

Ware, B. A. (2004). *God's Greater Glory*. Wheaton, IL: Crossway Books.

Watson, G. (2004a). Disordered Appetites. In *Agency and Answerability: Selected Essays* (pp. 59–87). Oxford: Clarendon Press.

Watson, G. (2004b). The Work of the Will. In *Agency and Answerability: Selected Essays* (pp. 123–59). Oxford: Clarendon Press.

Westphal, J. (2011). The Compatibility of Divine Foreknowledge and Freewill. *Analysis*, *71*(2), 246–52.

Widerker, D. (1987). On an Argument for Incompatibilism. *Analysis*, *47*(1), 37–41.

Widerker, D. (1990). Troubles with Ockhamism. *Journal of Philosophy*, *87*(9), 462–80.

Widerker, D. (1996). Contra Snapshot Ockhamism. *International Journal for Philosophy of Religion*, *39*(2), 95 102.

Wierenga, E. (2017). Omniscience. *Stanford Encyclopedia of Philosophy*. Retrieved from https://plato.stanford.edu/archives/spr2017/entries/omnis cience/.

Zagzebski, L. T. (1996). *The Dilemma of Freedom and Foreknowledge* (New edn). New York: Oxford University Press, USA.

Zagzebski, L. T. (2011). Eternity and Fatalism. In C. Tapp & E. Runggaldier (eds.), *God, Eternity, and Time* (pp.65–80). Farnham: Ashgate.

Funding Information

The authors acknowledge financial support from Augustana Research/Artistic Fund (summer stipend) and Sir John Templeton Foundation Grant No. #57397.

Cambridge Elements ≡

Philosophy of Religion

Yujin Nagasawa
University of Birmingham
Yujin Nagasawa is Professor of Philosophy and Co-director of the John Hick Centre
for Philosophy of Religion at the University of Birmingham. He is currently President
of the British Society for the Philosophy of Religion. He is a member of the Editorial
Board of *Religious Studies*, the *International Journal for Philosophy of Religion*
and *Philosophy Compass*.

About the Series
This Cambridge Elements series provides concise and structured introductions
to all the central topics in the philosophy of religion. It offers balanced, comprehensive
coverage of multiple perspectives in the philosophy of religion. Contributors
to the series are cutting-edge researchers who approach central issues in the philosophy
of religion. Each provides a reliable resource for academic readers and develops new
ideas and arguments from a unique viewpoint.

Cambridge Elements ≡

Philosophy of Religion

Printed in the United States
By Bookmasters